THE ELEMENTS OF DRAFTING

First edition	1946
Second edition	1951
Third edition	1959
Fourth edition	1968
Fifth edition	1976
second impression	1979
Sixth edition	1981
Seventh edition	1987
Eighth edition	1991
second impression	1994
Ninth edition	1995

SALES CENTRES AND AGENTS

HEAD OFFICE: 44-50 Waterloo Road NORTH RYDE NSW 2113
Tel: (02) 936 6444 Fax: (02) 888 2287

4th Floor 167 Phillip Street SYDNEY NSW 2000
Tel: (02) 235 0766 Fax: (02) 221 4004

568 Lonsdale Street MELBOURNE Vic 3000
Tel: (03) 670 7888 Fax: (03) 670 0138

1st Floor 40 Queen Street BRISBANE Qld 4000
Tel: (07) 221 6688 Fax: (07) 220 0084

9th Floor St George's Centre 81 St George's Terrace PERTH WA 6000
Tel: (09) 321 8583 Fax: (09) 324 1910

Sales Representative Bronte Elliott GPO Box 384 ADELAIDE SA 5001
Tel/Fax: (08) 295 7644 Mobile: 018 84 3052

Agent—Tony Nicholas Professional & Academic Books
1st Floor 42 Murray Street HOBART TAS 7000
Tel/Fax: (002) 248 882

NEW ZEALAND

Brooker's

Wellington   Auckland

CANADA

The Carswell Company Ltd
Ontario

HONG KONG

Bloomsbury Books Ltd

MALAYSIA

Malayan Law Journal Sdn Bhd

SINGAPORE

Butterworths Asia

UNITED KINGDOM

Sweet & Maxwell Ltd
London

USA

The Carswell Company Ltd
Ontario

Wm W Gaunt & Sons, Inc
Holmes Beach, Florida

Piesse

THE ELEMENTS
of
DRAFTING

NINTH EDITION

by

J K AITKEN

LL M (Melb)
A Barrister and Solicitor of the Supreme Court of Victoria
Formerly Independent Lecturer in Land Contracts
at the University of Melbourne

THE LAW BOOK COMPANY LIMITED
1995

Published in Sydney by

The Law Book Company Limited
44-50 Waterloo Road, North Ryde, NSW
568 Lonsdale Street, Melbourne, Victoria
40 Queen Street, Brisbane, Queensland
81 St George's Terrace, Perth, WA

National Library of Australia
Cataloguing-in-Publication entry

Aitken, J. K. (James K.).
    Piesse, the elements of drafting.

    9th ed.
    Bibliography.
    Includes index.
    ISBN 0 455 21320 8.

    1. Legal composition. 2. Law—Australia—Language. 3.
    Legal documents—Australia. 4. Contracts—Australia—
    Interpretation and construction. I. Piesse, E. L. (Edmund
    Leolin), 1880-1947. Elements of drafting. II. Title. III.
    Title: Elements of drafting.

808.06634

Designed and edited by Debbie Duncan
Typeset in Times Roman and Omega, 10 on 12 point, by Mercier
        Typesetters Pty Ltd, Granville, NSW
    Printed by Ligare Pty Ltd, Riverwood, NSW

Preface

In 1941, the University of Melbourne's Law School arranged for solicitors to give tutorial classes in drafting. Mr E L Piesse wrote a series of articles which were used as lecture notes by the tutors and were published in 1946 in their original form of addresses to the students.

Mr Piesse's criticisms of faults then evident in drafting and the advocacy by him and in successive editions of this book of more modern methods have helped to contribute to the simpler and more straightforward style of drafting in use today and to the discarding, to a marked extent, of old-fashioned terms and unnecessary legal jargon. This movement gained impetus from the publication in 1987 by the Victorian Law Reform Commission of its report Plain English and the Law. Because many practices recommended by this book have been widely adopted and those condemned have become less prevalent, the text has been substantially revised.

The principles of this book are of general application and remain important today notwithstanding great technological advances in the creation of documents. While ready intelligibility is an important and generally achievable quality, the basic test is that the document should be expressed with sufficient clarity to make it unnecessary to have recourse to rules of construction or decisions of the courts in order to find its meaning.

J K AITKEN

Melbourne
November 1994

Table of Contents

Table of Cases

Bibliography

Burrows, *Words and Phrases Judicially Defined* (Butterworth & Co Ltd, London, 1943).

Bythewood and Jarman, *System of Conveyancing* (3rd ed, 1841).

Coode, (George), *On Legislative Expression*. Extract from a Memorandum in the Report of the Poor Law Commissioners on Local Taxation to Her Majesty's Principal Secretary of State for the Home Department: House of Commons Papers, 1843, Vol xx. References in this book are to the pages of that volume.

Davidson, *Precedents and Forms in Conveyancing* (3rd ed, 1860-1880; 4th ed, Vol 1, 1874; Vol 2, Pt I, 1877; Vol 2, Pt II, 1881; 5th ed, Vol 1, 1885).

Dick, *Legal Drafting* (The Carswell Company Ltd, 1972).

Dickerson, (Reed), *The Fundamentals of Legal Drafting* (Little, Brown & Company, 1965).

Driedger, *The Composition of Legislation* (Queen's Printer and Controller of Stationery, Ottawa, 1957).

Freund, *Legislative Regulation* (The Commonwealth Fund, New York, 1932).

Garrow, *Law of Wills and Administration* (Wellington, New Zealand, 1932).

Hallett, (V G H), *Hallett's Conveyancing Precedents* (Sweet & Maxwell Ltd, London, 1965).

Halsbury, *Laws of England* (3rd ed, Butterworth & Co Ltd, London, 1960, Vol 37; 4th ed, Butterworth & Co (Publishers) Ltd, London, 1985, Vol 45).

Howe, *Pollock-Holmes Letters* (Cambridge University Press, 1942).

Key and Elphinstone, *Precedents in Conveyancing* (15th ed, Sweet & Maxwell Ltd, London, 1953).

Kimble, Joseph, *Drafting Documents in Plain Language* (Paper presented to Law Institute of Victoria, 1993).

Melville, *The Draftsman's Handbook* (Oyez Longman Publishing Ltd, London, 1985).

Norton on Deeds (2nd ed, Sweet & Maxwell Ltd, London, 1928).

Odgers, *Construction of Deeds and Statutes* (5th ed by Gerald Dworkin, Sweet & Maxwell Ltd, London, 1967).

Parker, *Modern Conveyancing Precedents* (Butterworth & Co Ltd, London, 1964).

Robinson, *Drafting* (Butterworth & Co (Publishers) Ltd, 1980).

Russell, (Sir Alison), *Legislative Drafting and Forms* (4th ed, Butterworth & Co Ltd, London, 1938).

Stroud, *Judicial Dictionary of Words and Phrases* (5th ed, Sweet & Maxwell Ltd, London, 1986).

Thornton, *Legislative Drafting* (Butterworth & Co Ltd, London, 1979).

Thring, (Lord), *Practical Legislation: The Composition and Language of Acts of Parliament and Business Documents* (John Murray, London, 1902).

Victorian Law Reform Commission, *Legislation, Legal Rights and Plain English*, Discussion Paper No 1 (1986).

Victorian Law Reform Commission, *Plain English and the Law*, Report No 9 (1987), including Drafting Manual.

1
Introduction

Taking instructions

The Elements of Drafting deals with expression rather than substance. But the subject to be dealt with is of necessity the first concern of a person who is required to draft a document. He or she must know what it is that the client wishes to achieve and must understand the transaction fully, both in its business relations and in its effects in law, before beginning to state these on paper.[1] A solicitor engaged in this task should either be familiar with the law which is relevant to the transaction or know where it can be found. Its business relations may be within the solicitor's experience or may be ascertained from the client but, in any case, the solicitor should be aware of them.

A solicitor's clients usually understand quite well the main relationship or result in business or law that they wish to bring about. They come to the solicitor partly because they wish to be safeguarded from the pitfalls of the law, but also because they wish the document they sign to be drawn with professional skill.

The professionally drawn document should embody accurately the client's instructions; it should be comprehensive, in the sense that it deals with all eventualities that should be covered; and it should be neither ambiguous, nor uncertain, nor vague. While material should never be included that is so vague or incomplete as to render it, or the whole document, void for uncertainty, the instructions of the client or the process of negotiation may result in some terms having a degree of imprecision. The client may prefer that an act should be done within a reasonable time rather than within a precisely stated period. The parties to a contract for the

---

1. "Before a draftsman can write a sentence he must know what he wants to say; and to find out what he wants to say is his most important and difficult problem": Driedger (1957), p 1.

1

sale of land may accept a stipulation that the contract should be conditional on the purchaser receiving by a stated date "approval for finance on satisfactory terms and conditions in an amount sufficient to complete the purchase". Time constraints or the circumstances may preclude the negotiation of a more specific provision. The provision quoted is undesirably vague, particularly for the vendor, but would probably not be held to be so uncertain as to be void. [2]

Another important and attainable quality is clarity, in the sense of being readily comprehensible to the audience to whom the document is primarily addressed.

Sometimes, while the solicitor is taking instructions, it is found that questions put to the clients assist them to a better understanding of the matter, and sometimes facts and possibilities are discovered not yet considered that must be referred to and the resulting legal rights and relationships agreed on and stated.

For instance, a client who wishes to leave his estate to his wife for life and then to his children may not have considered whether a child who dies before the wife is to share, or what is to be done if a child dies before the testator or the wife but leaves children who survive the testator and the wife. Again, he may not have thought of giving power to his wife to use capital in an emergency, such as a serious illness, or for a child's education or advancement during the wife's lifetime.

A solicitor advising the intending purchaser of a small business would draw attention to a number of matters which may not have occurred to the client, such as the time at which the purchaser will assume the risk for loss of or damage to the physical assets of the business; the desirability of restraining the vendor from competing with the purchaser for a specified period and within a specified area and the extent to which this can lawfully be done; and, where the business premises are leased, whether a mortgagee should be asked to consent to or confirm the assignment of the lease. These matters would be dealt with in a properly drawn agreement.

Language

It has been customary to criticise the length and complexity of legal documents and even to attribute this to greed. Although for

2. *Meehan v Jones* (1982) 56 ALJR 813.

some documents a lawyer is entitled to be paid in proportion to the number of words used, this applies only to a small part of a lawyer's work and, where it does apply, it would be quite unusual for redundant language to be used in order to augment fees. Length and complexity may be inherent in the nature of the transaction but can arise from following a traditional style of drafting (perhaps now better described as an old-fashioned style of drafting) and from an abundance of caution in seeking to cover every possible contingency. It has also been customary to criticise the use of legal jargon and of terms which are archaic or not often met with in everyday life.

This criticism has at times been justified. However, for 50 years or more, there has been a movement towards the adoption of a simpler and more modern terminology and the avoidance of archaic terms and towards the more efficient arrangement of material. Dickerson, in 1965, and subsequent writers,[3] strongly advocated these developments. Successive editions of this book have made similar recommendations.

Publication in 1987 by the Victorian Law Reform Commission of its report *Plain English and the Law*[4] gave an impetus to this trend.

The Commission recommends a more simple and straightforward drafting style. Plain English, the report states, "involves the use of plain straightforward language which . . . conveys its meaning as clearly and simply as possible, without unnecessary pretension or embellishment". The report is concerned with the drafting principally of legislation, but also of private legal documents. One of its general conclusions[5] is:

> **"The clarity of legal documents would be considerably improved if drafters got rid of these defects and adopted a plain English style in place of the present one. Plain English is not a special language. It is ordinary English, expressed directly and clearly to convey a message simply and effectively. It does not require the abandonment of technical terms or strict legal concepts."**

Ordinary words should be used, preferably short ones. A preference for Anglo-Saxon words over words of Latin origin is not justified except as a means of achieving simplicity of expression.

---

3. Dickerson (1965); Dick (1972); Robinson (1980).
4. Victorian Law Reform Commission, Report No 9.
5. Ibid, p xi.

The English language is derived from both sources and, if the word of Latin origin is more suitable, it should be used.

Russell's advice to the Parliamentary Draftsman applies to private documents:

> **"The simplest English is the best for legislation. Sentences should be short. Long words should be avoided. Do not use one word more than is necessary to make the meaning clear. The draftsman should bear in mind that his Act is supposed to be read and understood by the plain man. In any case he may be sure that if he can express his meaning in simple words all is going well with his draft: while if he finds himself driven to complicated expressions composed of long words it is a sign that he is getting lost and he should reconsider the form of the section."** [6]

The primary audience of a legal document consists of the people who will initially have recourse to it, for example, the general public in the case of consumer contracts, the shareholders of a company in the case of some corporate transactions, the proprietor, the architect and the builder in the case of a building agreement, the executors and the beneficiaries in the case of a will. There is a secondary audience that becomes significant where a dispute arises in connection with the document or doubt arises as to its meaning: the legal profession, courts and other tribunals. A great deal of study has gone into making legal writing readily intelligible to its primary audience. The avoidance of legal jargon and archaic words has been mentioned. Some writers have listed words and expressions the use of which should be avoided and have provided alternatives for them. English is a rich language. In addition to its Germanic origins, a considerable part of its vocabulary is derived from Latin, either directly or from French. There are borrowings from many other languages including Greek, Dutch, Italian and Spanish. If the precepts of plain English are followed, the creativity of the writer, the search for the correct word, need not be hampered by a requirement to eschew or adopt lists of proscribed and prescribed terms. The lists can be a useful guide.

Short sentences and short paragraphs are recommended as an aid to intelligibility. The meaning of a long sentence may be difficult

6. Russell (1938), p 12.

to grasp quickly or accurately. Some people may not be able to grasp it at all. The following sentence is taken from a covenant by the mortgagor to insure the mortgaged property. It is implied in mortgages registered under the *Victorian Transfer of Land Act* 1958[7] unless a contrary intention is shown:

> **That I my executors administrators or transferees will insure and so long as any money shall remain secured by this mortgage keep insured against loss or damage by fire in the name of the mortgagee or his transferees in some public insurance office to be approved by him or them all buildings fixtures or other improvements which shall for the time being be erected on the said land and which shall be of a nature or kind capable of being so insured to the amount of the principal money hereby secured or of the full value of such buildings and will where so required deposit with the mortgagee or his transferees the policy of such insurance and at least seven days before each premium is payable the receipt for such premium.**

This covenant is of a respectable age, having first appeared in the *Transfer of Land Statute* 1866. It is not easy to grasp its meaning on a first reading. It could be restated in two, possibly three, paragraphs. Several surplus words and expressions could be deleted. Several matters of substance should, perhaps, be dealt with to bring the covenant into conformity with today's practice: for instance, the risks to be insured against might extend beyond fire.

Legislation requiring documents relating to certain consumer transactions to achieve a standard of intelligibility has been enacted in some jurisdictions of the United States and has been enacted, but not widely, in Australia. As an example, the *Credit Act* 1984 (Vic)[8] provides that the Credit Licensing Authority may prohibit the use of certain documents found to be:

(a) expressed in language that is not readily comprehensible;

(b) written or printed in a colour, or on paper of a colour, that detracts from legibility of the document; or

(c) written or printed on a page in a style or manner that detracts from the legibility of the document.

Tests of readability based on such criteria as the average number of syllables to the word, average number of words to the sentence,

---

7. Section 75, Sched 15.
8. Section 152. See also ss 151 and 154.

average number of words to the paragraph are mechanical and are objective in the sense that they do not take account of the state of mind of the reader. Professor Kimble[9] recommends an average sentence length of 20 words or less. The view of the Victorian Law Reform Commission is that plain English laws should not impose objective tests.[10] The Commission also found that the need for a general plain English law had not been established.[11]

The drafter should use well constructed sentences which are as brief as practicable. Short sentences cannot always be used in legal documents. Circumstances, conditions, qualifications and exceptions may need to be stated and it may not be practicable to express them in a series of short sentences. A long sentence can be made more comprehensible by being set out in paragraphs and subparagraphs, each of which will begin a new line, and by the use of margins of varying width, as will be discussed below in Chapter 3.

The following example compares drafting in short sentences with the use of a single sentence. The testator is creating a trust by his will for the children of his sister and the children of deceased children of hers. His instructions can be reflected in sentences:

> **My estate is to be held in trust for my sister's present children in equal shares.**
> **If my sister has any more children who are born in my lifetime, they are to share.**
> **No child is to share who dies in my lifetime.**
> **No child or grandchild is to share unless he or she attains the age of 21 years.**
> **If a child of my sister dies before me and has one or more children who survive me and attain the age of 21 years, those children will take the share which the deceased parent would have taken if the parent had been alive at my death and had attained the age of 21 years and, if there is more than one of them, they are to share equally.**
> **If a child of my sister dies after me and is then under 21 years of age and has one or more children who survive that child and attain the age of 21 years, those children will take the share which the deceased parent would have taken if the parent had**

9. Kimble (1993), p 29.
10. Victorian Law Reform Commission, Report No 9, para 148.
11. Victorian Law Reform Commission, Report No 9, para 149.

been alive at my death and had attained the age of 21 years and, if there is more than one of them, they are to share equally.

This can be expressed in a single sentence which can be made more readable by minor subparagraphing:

My estate is to be held in trust in equal shares for such of the children of my sister as are alive at my death and attain the age of 21 years, but if any child of my sister:

(i) dies before me and has one or more children who survive me and attain the age of 21 years; or

(ii) is alive at my death, dies after me but before attaining the age of 21 years and has one or more children who survive that child and attain the age of 21 years,

then those children take, and if more than one in equal shares, the share which the deceased parent would have taken if that parent had attained a vested interest.

This is considerably shorter than the equivalent statement in separate short sentences, but it is more intricate and less easy to take in. It is a method more frequently used in wills, settlements and other documents relating to property for which the more intricate style tends to be followed and in the preparation and administration of which a solicitor will normally be involved.

Traditional forms

It was during the 18th century that lawyers' drafting reached its height of verbosity, both in statutes and in the work of conveyancers. A redundancy of language that would now be thought almost beyond endurance became common; and it has taken generations to cut it back. In the arrangement of parts of sentences there was intricacy and confusion. Bentham attacked the methods of expression used in statutes. His ideas were applied in George Coode's memorandum "On Legislative Expression", published in 1843 in a report of the Poor Law Commissioners on Local Taxation;[12] and this in turn helped in the shortening and simplifying of language that became more common in the statutes of about a century ago.

---

12. *House of Commons Papers* (1843), Vol XX. The memorandum is a model of exact reasoning and clear expression.

How far the change has gone in statutes can be seen if, for instance, the first section of a statute of importance in the history of Australia, the Act of 1784 for the transportation of offenders to places beyond the seas, which is an unbroken paragraph of over 50 lines containing about 800 words, is compared with a section of one of the early Acts of the Commonwealth, the *Customs Act 1903*, drawn by Mr R R Garran (later Sir Robert Garran) and Mr C C Kingston, an Act which is written in short sentences and arranged in short sections and subsections and paragraphs.

In relation to conveyancing practice, Davidson[13] remarked in 1874 of the redundancy of expression of an English conveyancer of the early part of the 18th century, James Booth, who has been called "the patriarch of the modern school of conveyancing", that it "long continued to infect our legal instruments". In the centuries that have elapsed since Booth's time, very much has been done to shorten legal documents and to make them clearer. But how much still remained possible will appear to anyone who compares Davidson's forms with those now in use. The qualities that distinguish the modern style of drafting—the use of definitions, division into numbered paragraphs and subparagraphs with marginal notes, the growing disuse of the form "shall" in stating circumstances and conditions, the use of one word (as "convey" or "assign") for the jumble ("grant, bargain, sell, alien, release, confirm and enfeoff" or "bargain, sell, assign, transfer, set over, and confirm") that had often previously been necessary, or thought to be so, are to be found in any modern set of precedents.

Davidson's form of conveyance of land by vendor to purchaser,[14] without description of the land, takes nearly 600 words. This can be compared with the short form of conveyance prescribed by statute[15] in most jurisdictions, or with the form of conveyance without recitals to be found in Key and Elphinstone's *Precedents*,[16] which contains less than 100 words.[17]

Not all of this simplification is due to any superior skill of modern drafters. It is the consequence in part of a change in the style of drafting, but in part also (particularly in the language of

---

13. Davidson (1874), Vol I, p 7.
14. Davidson (1877), Vol II, Pt I, p 229.
15. In Victoria, see *Property Law Act* 1958, Eighth Schedule. In New South Wales, see *Conveyancing Act* 1919, Second Schedule.
16. Key and Elphinstone (1953), Vol I, p 643.
17. Parker (1964), contains brief and simple forms.

documents relating to land) of changes in the law made by statute. For example, in modern forms of conveyance the use of the phrase "as beneficial owner" enables the language to be shortened because Parliament has enacted[18] that the phrase implies covenants for title which require over 500 words to set out at length.

Precedents

Legal practice relies on precedent. It would not be feasible for a busy solicitor to draft from the beginning a company's articles of association, a trust deed securing debenture stock or a bank mortgage. The precedent may embody modifications and improvements which reflect decades of experience. Many transactions are sufficiently stereotyped to enable a printed document or a standard form to be used: contracts of sale of land; Torrens system mortgages; leases of residential premises. Standard documents are convenient, for example, in the administration of a shopping centre or an office building for which a uniform lease may be evolved; or of a group of companies, the subsidiary companies in which may all have similar articles of association.

Precedents are available in a number of general and specialised publications and, in many areas of practice, are available commercially in electronic form. Firms can supplement and adapt precedents acquired externally or can develop their own precedents internally. Electronic storage of precedents facilitates their use in word processing equipment now in general use in legal offices.

Precedents should not be regarded as inflexible directions as to the words to be used. However closely the precedent may be followed, it is no more than a guide to the production of the document which fits the client's requirements and must be altered, added to and adapted accordingly. The drafter should understand the legal principles underlying a passage which is being used for a precedent. Slavish copying without such an understanding is dangerous; it is uncreative and does not provide the professional service to which the client is entitled.

A lawyer may do the client a disservice in failing to consult a precedent book where a suitable precedent is available. It will show

18. *Victorian Property Law Act* 1958, s 76. For further examples, see ss 62, 63, 64. *New South Wales Conveyancing Act* 1919, corresponding s 78; and ss 63, 67, 68.

the matters which are generally dealt with in a document of the kind contemplated. Such documents may follow a recognised form, or a statutory form, which it would be wise to adopt.

Computer aids to drafting

Improved computer equipment and software have greatly enhanced document creation since the introduction of word processing in Australia not much longer than 20 years ago. The drafting and production of documents has been facilitated and a lot of the drudgery involved has been eliminated. A supreme contribution of computers is their capacity to alter, add to and delete from documents and to revise them again and again with comparatively little trouble and without the need for the extensive checking that was once required.

In modern word processing, the operator has a choice of fonts, print can be italicised, made bold, increased or reduced in size; the layout of the document can be changed, margins varied, text centred or justified, the document displayed as it will appear when printed. The text can be checked for misspellings. Instances of a particular word or phrase can be identified and replaced. A thesaurus may be available whereby the operator can call up synonyms and antonyms for a selected word.

The power of word processors has been enhanced by data bases of elements from which a document may be created, consisting of libraries of precedents developed inhouse or acquired externally or by a combination of the two. For instance, a solicitor who has a library of will clauses can bring clauses up on the screen when taking instructions for a will. In one interview, it may be possible to settle the terms of the will and to print it as a draft or in its final form. If the client wishes to study the draft, it would be possible to execute a copy of it as an interim will.

Techniques have been developed whereby a precedent can be merged with information relating to the client and the matter to produce a complete document. In one reported instance,[19] a solicitor was asked at 4.30 pm on a Friday to produce a full set of documents for a real estate auction the next morning and was able to have them ready for the client to collect at 5 pm. Once the data

19. *Computers in the Law Office*, Property Law Bulletin (Vic) (June 1994).

base has been established, professional staff who do not have a high level of word processing skills are able to create their own documents.

This section is designed simply to give an indication of the electronic aids that are now available in drafting. We have come a long way from the time when clerks wrote legal documents with pen and ink, a laborious task, with no benign machine to wipe away and replace errors by one or two touches of its keyboard.

However, the most sophisticated equipment can do no more than carry out the commands issued to it. The author should not be seduced by the miraculous speed with which the document is produced nor by its attractive appearance from neglecting the important tasks of editing and checking the product. Drafting ability is required more than ever because of the increasingly complicated nature of our society and our economy.

2
General Principles

Intention of the parties

When a dispute arises about the construction of a document, lay-people will usually seek to determine it by reference to what they suppose, or claim, was the intention of the parties. But an inquiry as to intention will not be undertaken by the courts. The process of formation of intention is subjective and the determination of any common subjective intention, particularly where a number of people are concerned, is likely to be impracticable. The courts have decided that, in construing a document, they must ascertain "the expressed common intention"[1] of the parties. The rule has been stated:

> **"the question is not what the parties to a deed [or other document] may have intended to do by entering into that deed, but what is the meaning of the words used in that deed: a most important distinction in all cases of construction and the disregard of which often leads to erroneous conclusions."[2]**

And again: "But what a man intends and the expression of his intention are two different things. He is bound and those who take after him are bound by his expressed intention. If that expressed intention is unfortunately different from what he really desires, so much the worse for those who wish the actual intention to prevail."[3]

Agreements are no longer interpreted purely on internal linguistic considerations, isolated from the matrix of facts in which

1. *Groongal Pastoral Co v Falkiner* (1924) 35 CLR 157 at 162.
2. Lord Wensleydale in *Monypenny v Monypenny* (1861) 9 HLC 114 at 146; 11 ER 671; see further Odgers (1967), pp 27ff.
3. Sir Gorell Barnes P in *Simpson v Faxon* [1907] P 54. For a later statement of this doctrine by Lord Upjohn, see *Sefton v Tophams Ltd* [1967] AC 50 at 72.

they are set, as Lord Wilberforce said in *Prenn v Simmonds*.[4] Lord Wilberforce said that the court should examine the circumstances with reference to which the words were used and the object, appearing from those circumstances, which the person using them had in view; that evidence of mutually known facts was admissible to identify the meaning of a descriptive term; but that evidence of prior negotiations or of the parties' subjective intentions were not admissible.

In *Codelfa Construction Pty Ltd v State Rail Authority of New South Wales*,[5] Mason J (as he then was) said:

"**Consequently when the issue is which of two or more possible meanings is to be given to a contractual provision we look, not to the actual intentions, aspirations or expectations of the parties before or at the time of the contract, except in so far as they are expressed in the contract, but to the objective framework of facts within which the contract came into existence, and to the parties' presumed intention in this setting. We do not take into account the actual intentions of the parties and for the very good reason that an investigation of those matters would not only be time consuming but it would also be unrewarding as it would give too much weight to these factors at the expense of the actual language of the written contract.**"[6]

A mistake may result in clear words which prevail over any determination of intention.[7]

The need for accuracy in drafting is demonstrated by these rules. Calling evidence of circumstances or of mutually known facts in order to elucidate a document implies that its meaning is in the process of being ascertained by a court. The drafter has failed in her or his duty if an application to the court is needed to interpret or to rectify what has been written. The client who has to undergo the trouble, expense and delay of litigation has been poorly served.

4. [1971] 1 WLR 1381 at 1383-1384.
5. [1982] 149 CLR 337 at 352.
6. See M H Tobias QC, "Interpretation of Instruments" (1985) *Australian Bar Review* 126.
7. *National Society for the Prevention of Cruelty to Children v Scottish National Society for the Prevention of Cruelty to Children* [1915] AC 207. *Roddy v Fitzgerald* (1858) 6 HLC 823 at 876; 10 ER 1518, per Lord Wensleydale; *Re Smith* [1939] VLR 213 at 218, per O'Bryan J.

Likewise, the rectification of a contract to give effect to the actual intention of the parties or the implication of a term in a contract to give effect to the presumed intention of the parties will, unless the parties can come to an agreement, involve court proceedings.

In some Australian jurisdictions there has been amelioration of the rule that, in construing a will, the court is limited to ascertaining the meaning of what the testator has written.[8] Relief from the strict rule will involve an application to the court and the fact that such an application is needed may be a reflection on the drafter's competence.

Drafters must, therefore, understand the meaning which will be given by the courts to the words used. They must always be careful that the choice of words accurately reflects the intention of the client. They must never lose sight of the fundamental rule that the parties to a document will be presumed to have intended to say what they in fact have said, so that their words will be construed as they stand.

Combinations of facts

Because the intention of the parties to a document is gathered from the words used, it is essential that the drafter should think of all reasonable combinations of facts to which the words may be applied. No task is more difficult and none provides a greater justification for professional preparation of documents.

The need to be comprehensive is all the greater because courts do not readily supply terms which have been omitted from a contract. Apart from terms implied by law or usage in certain classes of transaction, a court will not import a missing term unless it complies with these rules:

(1) It must be reasonable and equitable;

(2) It must be necessary to give business efficacy to the contract, so that no term will be implied if the contract is effective without it;

(3) It must be so obvious that it goes without saying;

(4) It must be capable of clear expression;

(5) It must not contradict any express term of the contract.

8. In Victoria, *Wills Act* 1958, s 22A. In Queensland, *Succession Act* 1981, s 31 gives court power to rectify.

The drafter must be familiar with the terms that will be imported, unless excluded, and must include any required terms that will not be imported.[9]

An example of uncertainty which could have been avoided by stating a condition which a testator may, or may not, have intended to apply occurred in the South African case of *Kriel v Kriel*.[10] A will directed that unmarried daughters might reside in the family home with their brother, the legatee of it, and, if he married and the daughters decided to cease to reside there, he should make provision for their maintenance. Probably the testator assumed that the brother would continue to reside in the house, but he married and lived elsewhere. A daughter some time later decided to leave the family home and claimed maintenance. It was decided that the two conditions entitling the daughter to maintenance had occurred, namely the marriage of her brother and her leaving the family home. The drafter may have assumed that unmarried daughters would not leave unless the legatee married and continued to live at the house, but he did not provide expressly for this eventuality.

Basic drafting rules

Reasons for bringing legal documents into existence include:

to create, vary or negate legal rights and obligations;

to record legal rights and obligations;

by production of the document to a court or other tribunal, to enable those rights and obligations to be enforced or protected.

The basic rule is that of Lord Macaulay:

The first law of writing is that the words employed should be such as to convey to the reader the meaning of the writer.

Design of the Draft. Before beginning the draft, the whole design of it should be conceived. In the preparation of a will, for instance,

9. *Secured Income Real Estate (Australia) Ltd v St Martins Investments Pty Ltd* (1979) 144 CLR 596 at 606; *BP Refinery (Western Port) Pty Ltd v Hastings Shire Council* (1977) 52 ALJR 20 at 26; 16 ALR 363 at 376; *The Moorcock* (1889) 14 PD 64 at 68; *Reigate v Union Manufacturing Co* [1918] 1 KB 592.

10. (1948) (3) SA 309 (AD).

the drafter must decide whether the whole of the estate should be expressed to be vested in the executors (as does, in fact, happen after the testator's death) and all beneficial dispositions be directed to be made by the executors as trustees; or whether the will should simply set out the beneficial dispositions without making reference to the vesting of the estate in the executors. The drafter must also decide, if the former design is adopted, whether the executors will hold the estate in specie, possibly with a power of sale, on trust to carry out the testator's directions or will hold the estate on trust for sale and conversion into money.

> **"A general design, on which a considerable part of a draft has been drawn, should never be changed without urgent reason, because that part of the draft which has been previously prepared will, unless revised with anxious care, be inconsistent with the remainder, and will, in spite of every precaution, frequently retain discrepancies, in reference and otherwise, of a grave nature."** [11]

A security over a parcel of shares may take the form of a transfer of the shares to the lender or it may take the form of a charge over the shares, registered title to the shares remaining with the borrower. Having chosen the device of the transfer of the shares to the lender, it would be better to start again than to amend the draft so as to convert it to a charge over the shares without transfer.

The order of the draft should be logical. While opinions may differ as to the exact sequence required by strict logic, the nature of the transaction or the chronology of the events contemplated by the document, will indicate the order which is appropriate. In a mortgage, provisions dealing with the making and repayment of the loan and payment of interest would precede those dealing with default and the mortgagee's remedies.

In a building agreement, the order might be:

Agreement to build for the stipulated price;

Application for planning and building permits;

Insurance;

Construction;

Completion of the building;

11. Davidson (5th ed, 1885) by Wright & Darley, Vol I, Ch II, pp 15ff. The quotation is from Davidson (4th ed, 1874), Vol I, pp 20ff; similar remarks are made in the 5th ed.

Payment of the price;

Repair of defects found after completion;

Default or bankruptcy of proprietor or builder;

Reference of disputes to mediation or arbitration.

For a lease, this order might be chosen:

Grant of lease;

Term;

Rent and payment of rent;

Tenant's obligations;

Landlord's obligations;

Termination of lease on tenant's default;

Option to renew;

Machinery provisions such as service of notices.

Provisions relating to a particular topic, for example, mortgagee's remedies, should be grouped together and not scattered throughout the document. Mortgagee's remedies could be subdivided into several areas: personal action against the mortgagor; taking possession of the mortgaged property; deriving income by leasing; power of sale; appointment of receiver; foreclosure.

Nothing should be admitted or 'omitted unnecessarily. If unnecessary material is included that is not significant to the drafter, it is not likely to be intelligible to the reader. Every sentence, every word should have a job to do, should be included for a purpose.

Results which flow from the circumstances or are necessarily entailed do not normally need to be stated. If a grant of land is made to A and B as tenants in common, it is pointless to add "and not as joint tenants". In the event of an equality of votes, the chairperson of a meeting does not have a second or casting vote unless it is conferred on him by the regulations of the company or association.[12] Therefore, as a matter of drafting, it is unnecessary to provide that, in the case of an equality of votes, the chairperson shall *not* have a casting vote, in addition to a deliberative vote. However, because the regulations will be consulted during the conduct of meetings, the drafter may recommend to the client that

---

12. *Nell v Longbottom* [1894] 1 QB 767 at 771.

the superfluous provision should be included so that, if the question arises at a meeting, it can be promptly settled by reference to the regulations. This is a case where it is convenient to include a provision which may not be legally necessary.

Ordinary and accustomed forms and appropriate legal language should be employed. Where a form of instrument is accepted as effective for the purpose of bringing about or recording a class of transaction, it is convenient to use it. It will be familiar to the parties to the transaction and other persons connected with it and may reflect a settled commercial practice which should not be departed from without good reason. Again, unless there is reason to the contrary, the word which has become recognised as appropriate, whether by usage or from statutory origin, should be used: Torrens system land is "transferred", general law land is "conveyed", a chose in action is "assigned". The donor of a power of attorney can "revoke" it whereas the corresponding verb for a lease or an easement is to "surrender" it. To use other words with equivalent meanings would detract from the document's clarity and might cause difficulties of interpretation.

If the client wishes the document to reflect a statutory right or power or to reflect compliance with a statutory duty, the draft should follow the words of the statute. Under s 30 of the *Trustee Act* 1958 (Vic) a trustee who is about to depart from Victoria may by power of attorney delegate to any person the execution or exercise while he is out of Victoria of all or any of the trusts powers and discretions vested in him as trustee. If a trustee who was about to go abroad wished to delegate to an attorney the widest possible powers, the grant should be worded: "to execute and exercise while I am out of Victoria all the trusts powers and discretions vested in me as trustee of the . . ."

Drafter's Golden Rule—Don't change the language unless you wish to change the meaning.

"Never change your language unless you wish to change your meaning, and always change your language if you wish to change your meaning"—the drafter's "golden rule"—is a statement in simpler language of the two errors condemned by Bentham:

"Unsteadiness in respect of expression: when for the description of the same import, divers words or phrases are employed.

Unsteadiness in respect of import: when to the same word or phrase, divers imports are attached in different places."

Avoidance of these errors lies at the root of all accurate expression in legal documents. A person or thing should always be called by the same name and a circumstance or condition or result should be described, when referred to again, in the same words; the same word should never be used for different circumstances or conditions or results.

If the subject matter of a lease has been described as "the leased premises" it should, throughout the document, be called "the leased premises" and not "the demised premises" or "the leased property". Having referred to the object of a gift as "the legatee", she should not later be called "the beneficiary". "On the cessation of her employment" and "on the termination of her employment" should not both be used if the same thing is meant. If both expressions are used, the latter might be interpreted as being restricted to termination by the act of the employer or the employee.

The precision that nowadays is ensured by using a descriptive word in an invariable sense used to be attained by repeating the original words of reference with the word "said" or "aforesaid". For instance, if John William Adolphus Brown and Herbert Frederick Norman Jackson were mentioned, and they had to be mentioned again, then, every time this happened, the drafter would write "the said John William Adolphus Brown and the said Herbert Frederick Norman Jackson". Nowadays John William Adolphus Brown and Herbert Frederick Norman Jackson would be referred to by their names alone, without the addition of "the said" which would not normally be required to distinguish them, or by some descriptive term such as "the Purchasers", "the Borrowers" or whatever might be appropriate: see below, Chapter 5.

Application of the golden rule eliminates use of the device of elegant variation of language. This device has no place in the drafting of legal documents. Elegance must be sacrificed to precision and clarity. The fact that the draft does not read smoothly or that words and expressions are repeated in identical form, thus detracting from its literary merit, is immaterial so long as it embodies the client's instructions, accurately and clearly.

Intelligibility of documents

Even if these rules are applied in the drafting of a document, it will not necessarily be readily intelligible to a lay-person. This does not mean that the drafter is at fault. A legal document must be precise and accurate and comprehensive and, if it is to have these qualities, it may have to be expressed in language which must be studied carefully by the reader in order to be understood. Where the subject matter is complex or technical, it may be even more difficult to follow: it may require deeper concentration and may not be fully comprehended without knowledge of the subject matter's technicalities. The drafter's audience, the client and those with whom the client is dealing, will probably have this knowledge. The drafter should aim to make the document as intelligible as is practicable and to reach its audience.

Organisation of material and logical arrangement, layout and typography, are aids to understanding. Short sentences are more readily comprehended. Sentences may be long if circumstances, conditions, exceptions and qualifications need to be included. Long sentences will sometimes be unavoidable. They are easier to follow if paragraphed as recommended below in Chapter 3.

3
Drafting in Paragraphs

Former use of single continuous sentences

Legal documents used to be handwritten in one compact mass, each line stretching from margin to margin, without a space to catch the eye, and no more help to picking out the several parts than could be got from an occasional word written in legal text, or a capital letter or word underlined. Sentences were very long and sometimes the whole of a document was constructed grammatically as a single continuous sentence. Lines written across a skin of parchment might be half a metre long. The mighty deeds of the early conveyancers had physical obstacles to their understanding as well as those that came from their language.

Reasons for the unbroken lines from margin to margin may have been to save parchment and to leave no space for a fraudulent addition. Modern documents, written electronically or by machine in place of hand, and often with ample blank space, certainly make alteration and addition easier than they used to be, as do modern methods of erasure and photocopying. Nevertheless, it is very unusual to hear of a typewritten document having been fraudulently altered.

Documents such as the old deeds are now rare but long passages of uninterrupted text are still encountered.

Splitting into paragraphs

One of the most useful aids to clearness of statement, bringing the eye to the aid of the understanding, is to split into short paragraphs a long sentence or a series of long sentences unbroken by the setting in of a line to catch the eye. ("Paragraph" is not used in the sense of a distinct section but to refer to a passage which commences on a new line and ends without running on to the next passage.)

This is the method commonly used in statutes, when statements are grouped in one clause rather than several clauses. The statement of the matter to which the clause applies, together with conditions and exceptions, may make a very long and intricate sentence, if all are joined in one. The complexity can be broken down, and the eye brought to the aid of the mind if, in place of a single continuous sentence, a series of short passages is used and these arranged as numbered or lettered paragraphs, each beginning a new line.

Arrangement of paragraphs

The arrangement of paragraphs can take two main forms.

A number having been given to the clause, the sentences that are to make up the clause can be arranged in subclauses numbered, say (1), (2), etc. An alternative is to commence the clause with an introductory passage on which the remaining material can depend and then to set out the remaining material in paragraphs numbered or lettered, say (a), (b), etc. In the latter method the continuity of the single sentence is retained and the paragraphs, although given distinctive letters, can be read as parts of the single sentence.

An example of drafting in *subclauses*:

(1) On a show of hands every person who is a shareholder or a shareholder's representative appointed under s 249 of the Corporations Law has one vote.

(2) On a poll every shareholder present in person or by proxy or attorney or by a representative appointed under s 249 of the Corporations Law has one vote for every share of which that shareholder is registered as the holder.

This passage, another example of the use of paragraphs, describes the date on which a settlement may be wound up and the assets distributed amongst the beneficiaries:

The Vesting Date means the first to occur of the following dates:

(i) such date earlier than 30 June 1998 as the Trustee may, with the consent of the Settlor, appoint;

(ii) such date not earlier than 30 June 1998 but not later than 29 June 2008 as the Trustee may appoint; and

(iii) 30 June 2008.

The last two paragraphs should be joined by *and* or *or*, as the sense requires, except in the case of a list:

The names of the shareholders and their shareholdings are:

John Smith	**5000 shares**
William Jones	**2000 shares**
Helen Johnson	**2500 shares**

A clause found in leases and designed to deal with the contingency of destruction of or damage to the leased premises occurring during the term often takes the form of a single continuous sentence. It is more easily comprehended if divided into subclauses, paragraphs and subparagraphs:

(1) **If, during the term of this lease, the leased building is destroyed or so damaged by fire flood storm tempest lightning or other cause beyond the control of the Tenant as to be unfit for occupation by the Tenant:**

    (a) (i) **subject to subparagraph (ii), at the election of either the Landlord or the Tenant, the term of this lease will determine;**

       (ii) **the election shall be in writing, shall be served on the other party not later than 30 days after the occurrence of the destruction or damage and shall take effect at the expiration of 14 days after the day of its service on the Landlord or the Tenant (as the case requires);**

    (b) **if neither party determines the term of this lease under paragraph (a):**

       (i) **the Landlord shall, as soon as is reasonably practicable after the destruction or damage, and at the Landlord's expense, reinstate the leased building;**

       (ii) **the rent or a fair proportion of it according to the nature and extent of the destruction or damage will, from the occurrence of the destruction or damage and until the leased building has been reinstated, and made fit for occupation, cease to be payable.**

(2) **Any difference between parties under this clause and, in particular, any difference concerning the proportion or the**

period of the abatement of rent under subparagraph (1)(b)(ii), shall be referred to arbitration in accordance with the provisions of the Commercial Arbitration Act 1984.

Each paragraph, when read alone with common introductory matter, and any intermediate and concluding matter, should make an intelligible grammatical sentence, as in this example:

A right, privilege or obligation of a person by reason of that person's membership of the Association:

> **is not capable of being transferred or transmitted to another person; and**
> **terminates upon the cessation of her or his membership.**

The drafter may adopt any system of lettering or numbering for clauses, subclauses and other subdivisions. Whatever system is adopted should be consistently applied throughout the document. Subclauses should not be designated (1), (2), (3), etc in one clause and (a), (b) and (c) in another. The same pattern should be adhered to.

The various parts of the document can be designated by letters and by Arabic and Roman numerals, bracketed or unbracketed. The system commonly adopted is a useful guide:

Clauses—Arabic numerals: 1, 2, etc.

Subclauses—bracketed Arabic numerals: (1), (2), etc.

Paragraphs—bracketed small letters: (a), (b), etc.

Subparagraphs—bracketed small Roman numerals: (i), (ii), etc.

Sub-subparagraphs—bracketed capital letters or capital Roman numerals: (A), (B), etc or (I), (II), etc.

Where paragraphs depend on an introductory passage, they are conventionally designated (a), (b), etc and subparagraphs and sub-subparagraphs are designated as above.

Instead of distinguishing parts of a document by letters, Arabic and Roman numerals and brackets, a "decimal" system may be used. If the principal division is into clauses, each clause can be given a number. For the next order of subdivision, say subclause, a decimal point is placed after the clause number and followed by the number of the subclause, and so on for further orders of subdivision. Paragraph 3 of subclause 2 of Clause 14 would be represented by 14.2.3. If the document is long, it can be divided into parts which can be distinguished by capital letters or by name, for example, B or "Preparation of Tender" and the decimal system used in each part: "B 6.4.2" or "Preparation of Tender 6.4.2". The decimal system facilitates typing.

Division into parts and successive subdivision of those parts should not be carried too far. A stage will be reached where the structure of the clause becomes so complex that it detracts from the clarity and ease of communication which paragraphing is meant to achieve. When this happens, the material should be re-arranged. Robinson[1] says that paragraphing where the paragraphs depend on an introductory passage should go no further than the level of sub-subparagraph.

The drafter should be regular in the use of margins for each of the various grades of division. This is important because failure to do so may make the meaning doubtful or different from what was intended.

This clause of a company's articles of association consists of one long sentence:

A director may hold any office or place of profit under the Company (other than that of auditor) and may enter into any contract with the Company either as vendor, purchaser or otherwise, and no such contract and no contract, transaction or arrangement, entered into by or on behalf of the Company in which a director is interested shall be avoided nor shall a director be disqualified from being a director by holding any such office or place of profit or being interested in any such contract, transaction or arrangement nor shall he be liable to account to the company for any profit arising from such office or place of profit or realised by any such contract transaction or arrangement by reason only of the director holding the office or place of profit or the fiduciary relationship thereby established and the director may not vote at a meeting of the Board in respect of any matter in which he is interested but may be counted in the quorum for the meeting.

It can be divided into subclauses and paragraphs and is then easier to apply to a particular situation.

1. Robinson (1980), p 50.

(1) A director may:

  (a) hold any office or place of profit under the Company (other than that of auditor);

  (b) enter into any contract with the Company either as vendor purchaser or otherwise.

(2) By reason of a director holding an office or place of profit under the Company or the fiduciary relationship thereby established:

  (a) he shall not be disqualified from being a director;

  (b) no contract by the director with the Company nor any contract transaction or arrangement entered into by or on behalf of the Company in which the director is interested shall be avoided;

  (c) the director shall not be liable to account to the Company for any profit arising from any such office or place of profit or realised from any such contract transaction or arrangement.

(3) A director may not vote at a meeting of the Board in respect of any matter in which he is interested but he may be counted in the quorum for the meeting.

Cross reference

Where a document is divided into clauses, the clauses into subclauses and the subclauses into paragraphs, they should be referred to in a consistent manner, that is, the same subdivision, or subdivisions of the same status, should not be referred to as a paragraph on one occasion and as a subclause on another. When referring to a paragraph one can say "paragraph (b) of subclause (3) of clause 4". This method of reference is too lengthy and it is preferable to refer to clause 4(3)(b), or more correctly, perhaps, to paragraph 4(3)(b), but each of them is quite clear and either usage is acceptable.

Reference in a document, say an agreement, to "clause 4" will, except in unusual circumstances, be read as a reference to clause 4 of the agreement itself. It will rarely be necessary to add "of this agreement". Similarly, reference in a clause to a subclause, such as "in accordance with subclause (2)" or "subject to subclause (5)" will be taken to refer to a subclause of that same clause without the addition of the words "of this clause".

Paragraphs facilitate statement of exceptions, conditions, etc

The advantage that drafting in paragraphs affords is in part the opportunity for division and subdivision into short sentences, or parts of sentences, each standing out clearly to the eye because it commences a new line, and in part the freedom of arrangement and the ease with which an exception or qualification that refers only to one of several particulars can be isolated and its application made clear.

Exceptions

Where a general provision does not apply in certain circumstances, a drafter in the old-fashioned style would, after the general statement, add "Provided that" and state the exception.

This usage is one of the instances Coode[2] gives of the misuse of the proviso.[3] He says that exceptions should not be expressed by a proviso but as exceptions:

> **where the enunciation of the general provision is merely to be negatived in some particular, the proper place for the expression of that negation is by an exception expressed in immediate contact with the general words by which the particular would otherwise be included.**

This object is easily achieved when the sentence is set out in separate paragraphs; the exception is then made part of the paragraph to which it applies. Or, if the exception affects the clause as a whole, it can be stated in a self-contained subclause or paragraph.

A lease is to contain a covenant which restricts the tenant from assigning subletting or parting with possession of the leased premises without the prior consent in writing of the landlord. The tenant is one of a group of related companies and the parties have agreed that the lease may be freely assignable to other companies in the group. If the method criticised by Coode were followed, the covenant would be set out and this proviso would be added:

> **Provided that this covenant shall not apply to an assignment of the lease to a body corporate which is related to the Tenant within the meaning of s 50 of the Corporations Law.**

2. Coode (1843), p xxv.
3. See below, p 86.

An alternative is to include the exception in the body of the covenant in proximity to the passage affected and, by paragraphing, make the meaning clear:

The Tenant may not without the consent in writing of the Landlord:

   (i) assign this lease, except to a body corporate which is related to the Tenant within the meaning of s 50 of the Corporations Law; or

   (ii) sublet or part with possession of all or any part of the premises.

Conditions and qualifications

When there are conditions or qualifications, sometimes the method of the continuous sentence, with paragraphs within it, is more convenient, and sometimes the method of several subclauses or paragraphs, each a complete sentence in itself. As with an exception, if there is a qualification to the operation of the clause as a whole, we may use the method of the continuous sentence commencing with introductory words and divided into paragraphs. This may be the safer course because, in a continuous sentence, even if it is set out in paragraphs, the qualification is unlikely to be masked. If the method of division into subclauses, each complete as a sentence in itself, is chosen, the effect of the qualification may be brought out in the main operative subclause by such a phrase as "Subject to subclause (--)".[4]

A settlor wishes the trustees to have power to invest in shares and other securities but subject to an exception and a qualification. The exception is placed near the relevant material in subclause (1) and the qualification, which affects the power generally, is placed in a separate subclause (2). The opening words of subclause (1) warn that subclause (2) must be considered in relation to the investment power.

(1) Subject to subclause (2), the Trustees may invest the Trust Fund in shares, stock units, debentures, debenture stock, notes, convertible notes, units in a unit trust or other securities which are officially quoted under the listing rules applying to any stock exchange in Australia, except securities of a

---

4. See below, p 89.

corporation or trust principally engaged in mining or oil production or in prospecting or exploring for oil or other minerals.

(2) Before making an investment under the power conferred by subclause (1), the Trustees shall obtain and consider the advice of a member of the Australian Stock Exchange Limited.

A simple example follows of the use of paragraphs, and the punctuation that is suitable, when the form of a continuous sentence is used to specify particulars to which different conditions attach:

Any person employed by the company shall be deemed to become a member:

(a) if on 1 August, 1994, that person was so employed and had been so employed continuously for a period of six months and had on or before that date attained the age of 21 years—on 1 August, 1994; or

(b) in any other case—on 1 August next following the date on which that person completes six months' continuous employment by the company.

Arrangement of particulars in their natural order

The use of paragraphs also shows clearly the order of the arrangement of particulars, which should be their natural order. For conditions, the natural order is that of their performance, for if this is used it will often be found that one throws light on the next; for actions or events the natural order is that of their succession in time.

An example of the natural order of conditions:

If an applicant:

(a) has attained the age of 21 years,

(b) has completed six months' service, and

(c) agrees to be bound by this Trust Deed,

she may be accepted as a member.

An example of events not arranged in their natural order:

The office of treasurer shall be vacated if she:

(a) dies, or

(b) becomes bankrupt, or

(c) has completed three years in office.

4
Arrangement and Order

Legal writing should be an effective communication of the author's meaning to the reader without undue concentration or effort by the latter. The use of short sentences and, where a long sentence is unavoidable, the device of paragraphing described above in Chapter 3 are ways of improving readability. Another important method is the right arrangement of the parts of sentences.

Documents relating to consumer transactions should be made easy to read: agreements for the acquisition or hiring of goods or services for personal or household use; borrowing money or obtaining credit at the retail level; fire or motor car or life insurance policies; residential tenancy agreements; even contracts for the sale or purchase of domestic housing.

George Coode, in 1843, reacting against the turgid style in which statutes were then drafted, said in discussing the elements and form of the legislative sentence:

> **"nothing is more required than that, instead of an accidental and incongruous style, the common popular structure of plain English should be resorted to."**[1]

Coode analyses the legislative sentence. His remarks apply also to sentences in contracts by which the parties regulate their rights and duties, and to other private legal documents.

Coode says that no law can be written without a legal subject, being a person who is commanded or permitted to perform, or is prohibited from performing, a legal action, and the legal action itself which is commanded, permitted or prohibited. Where the law is of constant and universal application, the legal sentence may consist of these two elements alone:

Thou shalt not steal;

1. *Language of Statutes, Verbs*, Coode (1843).

Thou shalt not bear false witness against thy neighbour.

The legal subject may be disguised or kept out of view: "No parking", but laws must be addressed to persons, either natural persons or juristic persons, entities which are persons in the eye of the law in that they have rights and duties and can sue and be sued.

Coode points out that the legal action is often to take place only in defined circumstances or on defined occasions, "the case", in which the peremptory provisions of the sentence are to operate:

When the term of the lease ends, the Tenant must remove her fixtures and other property from the leased premises and make good any damage caused by their removal.

A law or other imperative provision whether or not restricted as to the persons to which it is to apply and whether or not restricted to defined occasions or circumstances (cases), may still operate only on the performance of certain conditions:

If the Tenant gives the Landlord, not less than three months before the expiration of the term of this lease, notice in writing of her intention to renew this lease for a further term of two years, she shall be entitled to a renewed lease for the further term of two years.

Coode says that the full legislative sentence, embodying one or more cases and conditions, can take this form and its four elements should be placed in this order:

(1) the *case* or circumstances with respect to which or the occasion on which the sentence is to take effect;

(2) the *condition*,[2] what is to be done to make the sentence operative;

(3) the *legal subject*, the person enabled or commanded to act; and

(4) the *legal action*, that which the subject is enabled or commanded to do.

One of his instances is:

(1) (*case*) Where there is any question between any parishes touching the boundaries of such parishes;

2. In other passages in this work *case* and *condition* are used in these meanings, namely *case* (in relation to the structure of a sentence) as meaning the occasion or circumstances on which or with respect to which the sentence is to take effect, and *condition* as meaning what is to be done to make the sentence operative.

(2) (*condition*) if a majority of not less than two thirds in number and value of the landowners of such parishes make application in writing;

(3) (*legal subject*) the Tithe Commissioners for England and Wales;

(4) (*legal action*) may deal with any dispute or question concerning such boundaries.

The same elements may be found in a regulation in a company's articles of association:

(1) (*case*) Where, in the winding up of the company, assets are available for distribution among the members;

(2) (*condition*) if the members, by special resolution, sanction the disposition of those assets in kind;

(3) (*legal subject*) the liquidator;

(4) (*legal action*) shall divide those assets in kind among the members in proportion to their shareholdings.

The order—(1) case, (2) condition, (3) subject, (4) action

Coode's advice[3] is that a legislative sentence should be arranged in the order used in these examples, namely:

(1) case,

(2) condition,

(3) legal subject,

(4) legal action.

It is sometimes difficult to decide whether an element of a legal sentence is to be characterised as case or condition and it is not necessary that both or either of them be present. Take this provision in a contract of sale of real estate:

If the purchaser fails to pay the residue of purchase money on the Completion Date, he shall pay interest on the residue of purchase money at the rate of 12 per cent per annum.

The subordinate clause commencing "If" is best characterised as a condition because it describes an event under human control

3. Coode (1843), p xix.

which triggers the legal action. It could be said that the "case" is implicit: "Where under this contract the purchaser has agreed to pay the residue of purchase money on the Completion Date". However, not all sentences fit Coode's specification or can be fitted into it by expressing an implicit set of circumstances in which the sentence will take effect. Sentences can take a great variety of forms.[4] A sentence which is rational and acceptable may not have a person as its grammatical subject:

A notice may be given by the company to the joint holders of a share by giving the notice to the joint holder who is named first on the register of members.

Coode's advice will often be a guide to framing sentences in private legal documents. Such sentences have a logical internal order and this helps to convey the meaning. His advice is not of univeral application. Where the sentence is split into paragraphs, it may be convenient to vary the order. Improving the readability of the sentence, or its impact on the reader, both important considerations, may suggest that a different style should be adopted.

This is an example of an association's rule under which its governing body may relieve a member from expulsion for non-payment of subscriptions:

The committee may determine the manner in which a member who has been prevented by special circumstances from paying arrears of subscription and who, within two months of receiving a letter from the association requiring payment of the arrears, gives notice in writing of those circumstances to the secretary may retain membership otherwise than by paying all arrears of subscription.

If the formula recommended by Coode is applied the rule would be worded as follows and would be clearer:

Where a member has been prevented by special circumstances from paying arrears of subscription, if the member, within two months after receiving a letter from the association requiring payment of the arrears, gives notice in writing of those circumstances to the secretary, the committee may determine the manner in which the member may retain membership otherwise than by paying up all arrears of subscription.

4. Thornton (1979), pp 23-25.

The statement of the case or circumstances can commence with *when* or *where*, these words having no reference to time or place but meaning "if the following circumstances exist"; either of these words makes a convenient distinction between the commencement of the case and the commencement of a condition; for the latter *if* (or, to introduce a negative or a time limit, *unless* or *until*) is suitable. Russell[5] recommends that "where" should be used if frequent recurrences of the event are contemplated; "when" if only a single or rare occurrence is contemplated.

Examples are:

Where an individual executes a deed he shall either sign or place his mark upon the same and sealing alone shall not be deemed sufficient.[6]

Where the purchaser defaults in payment of a monthly instalment, she shall pay interest on the amount of instalment.

When any department of the public service of a State becomes transferred to the Commonwealth, all officers of the department shall become subject to the control of the Executive Government of the Commonwealth.[7]

When the purchaser pays the residue of purchase money, she becomes entitled to possession of the land.

Coode recommends that the indicative mood be used for the case and the subjunctive or conditional for the condition. The subjunctive and, to a less extent, the conditional, is being replaced in speech and writing by the indicative. The use of the indicative mood for both the case and the condition will nearly always be suitable.[8]

Beginning with a reason, condition or exception

As mentioned, Coode's recommended arrangement cannot always be conveniently followed. A sentence that states the reason for what it provides is sometimes clearer if the reason is put first. For example:

The trustees may, in their absolute discretion, surrender, cancel or otherwise deal with any benefit that under the

5. Russell (1938), p 117.
6. *Property Law Act* 1958 (Vic), s 73(1).
7. *Commonwealth of Australia Constitution Act* 1901, s 84.
8. See also below, pp 68-69.

Scheme is provided for the member, so as to obtain reimbursement of the amount unpaid by him.

This may be re-arranged:

To enable the trustees to obtain reimbursement of the amount unpaid by a member, they may, in their absolute discretion, surrender, cancel or otherwise deal with any benefit provided for him under the Scheme.

Beginning with principal clause

Coode's order is logical. It may not be the most effective means of communication. If the drafter's intention is to have an immediate impact on the reader, a sentence in which the principal clause comes first and is followed by the conditional clauses may be more easily understood.[9] Compare:

The Lender will accept interest for a quarter year at a rate which is 2 per cent per annum lower than the prescribed rate if the Borrower pays the interest within seven days of the due date and is not otherwise in breach of this agreement.

with

If the Borrower pays interest for a quarter year within seven days of the due date and is not otherwise in breach of this agreement the Lender will accept interest for that quarter year at a rate which is 2 per cent per annum lower than the prescribed rate.

Most modern statutes contain sections which begin by stating that the rule laid down is subject to conditions or to exceptions. The main advantage of this construction, both in statutes and in commercial and other documents, is that the condition or exception is immediately apparent, however hurriedly the provision is read. For instance, s 74 of the *Commonwealth of Australia Constitution Act* provides:

Except as provided in this section, this Constitution shall not impair any right which the Queen may be pleased to exercise by virtue of Her Royal Prerogative to grant special leave of appeal.

9. Victorian Law Reform Commission, Discussion Paper No 1, p 18.

An example of a paragraph beginning with an exception is given in Key and Elphinstone's *Precedents*,[10] where a special condition of sale reads, "*With the exception of the expense of making and delivering the abstract*, all expenses whatsoever . . . of and incidental to the verification or completion of the abstract, or the investigation or proof of the title," etc, shall be paid by the purchaser.

Reference in one provision of a document to other provisions which contain qualifications or exceptions makes the document easier to understand and may resolve inconsistencies. Article 60 of a company's articles of association provides that all shareholders may vote at a general meeting. Article 3, which creates preference shares, provides that the voting rights of the holders of those shares are restricted. Article 60 can begin: "Subject to the restriction in Article 3 on the voting rights of the holders of preference shares . . ." This passage not only refers the reader to Art 3 but shows that Art 3 prevails over Art 60 on the question of voting rights.

The Victorian Law Reform Commission's Drafting Manual[11] refers to the average sentence length of 20 to 25 words recommended by some writing manuals and adds:

If writers find that they are exceeding this limit, especially when the material is complicated, then they should check their sentences. The structure may be unduly complex.

The manual discusses the device of putting the principle clause first and points out that if the principal clause is preceded by a number of conditional clauses, readers will have difficulty interpreting them until the principal clause is reached. As it points out, this is no problem for the drafters because they know the solution before they write; but the general readers do not know it.

The manual recommends against interposing lengthy material between an auxiliary verb and the main verb or between the subject and the verb: framing a sentence in this way may make it difficult to take in.

To facilitate reading, material which relates back to material in the previous sentence can be placed at the beginning of the new sentence, thus linking it with what has gone before, and giving greater emphasis to the new material which will be placed at the end.[12]

10. Key and Elphinstone (1953), Vol 1, p 418.
11. pp 33-37, paras 70-77.
12. Kimble (1993), pp 42 et seq.

Whatever arrangement is adopted for the legal sentence it should be clear and effective and, so far as practicable, should assist the reader to a ready understanding of it. When preparing a legal document, the drafter should remember that the client may wish to exercise the rights or enforce the obligations which it creates. The document must point clearly to the person who is to perform or is to observe these obligations. This can be done by using the active voice: "The Secretary shall keep a register of the members". The passive voice can cause difficulties—a provision in a lease: "The leased premises will be kept in repair" does not say whether the landlord or tenant is to keep the premises in repair. The doubt may or may not be resolved by the context. [13]

When examining the draft, the author can test its efficacy by framing a statement of claim based on a hypothetical breach of duty by a party.

Where one party is required to serve a notice or take some other step in order to have a right or exercise a remedy against the other, the document should show clearly how the notice is to be worded and how it is to be served. This option to renew a lease does not give the tenant a guide to the form of notice or, in fact, to the procedure to be adopted in order to renew the lease:

The tenant, having given the landlord notice in writing at any time prior to the expiration of the term of this lease, shall have an option to renew this lease for a further term of five years, at the same rent and on the same terms and conditions as are contained in this lease except for this option of renewal.

Adjectives qualifying two or more nouns. Ambiguity

Modern English is not highly inflected. Syntax, or the arrangement of words in a sentence by which their connection and relation are shown, is more important in English than in a language such as Latin where the connection and relation between words is shown by their inflections. The drafter must ensure that the order of the words of the sentence enables the intended meaning to be expressed and that the order chosen does not conceal an ambiguity.

13. See below, p 92.

In arranging the structure of a sentence a problem frequently arises when an adjective, adjectival phrase or adjectival clause is used which is intended to qualify a number of particulars. The simplest instance is of an adjective preceding a number of particulars joined by "or". If one writes "charitable institutions or organisations", does one mean "charitable institutions or *any* organisations" or only "charitable institutions or *charitable* organisations"? According to the ordinary use of English the latter is meant and it was so held in *Re Griffiths*.[14] Another example is to be found in the Scottish case *Cameron's Trustees v Mackenzie*[15] where a gift was made to "charitable institutions, persons, or objects" to be selected by trustees, and it was decided that the adjective "charitable" governed persons and objects as well as institutions. The distinction was important because at that time a trust in favour of entities which could be selected by the trustees and which might not be charitable in the legal sense failed for uncertainty. The distinction is still important but ameliorating legislation has been enacted in many Australian jurisdictions.[16]

But if, besides the connective, there is a word qualifying the second member—as in the phrase "charitable institutions or voluntary organisations"—there may be doubt. So, in the Scottish case of *Symmers' Trustees v Symmers*,[17] trustees were directed to divide residue among "such charitable institutions or deserving agencies as they may select". It was held that the bequest failed because the description "deserving agencies" had to be read separately from "charitable institutions" and so the bequest was not exclusively charitable. If the organisations intended to be benefited by a gift are any, whether charitable or not, the arrangement "voluntary organisations or charitable institutions" is free from doubt; if the organisations are those only that are charitable, repeat the word charitable, as "charitable institutions or voluntary charitable organisations", or use the form "institutions or voluntary organisations (the institutions and organisations being charitable)".

14. [1926] VLR 212.
15. 1915 SC 313.
16. Vic: *Property Law Act* 1958, s 131. NSW: *Conveyancing Act* 1919, s 37D. Qld: *Trusts Act* 1973, s 104. SA: *Trustee Act* 1936, s 69a. WA: *Trustees Act* 1962, s 102.
17. 1918 SC 337.

If there is a *qualifying phrase or clause that follows the last member* there is again doubt for the courts, unless there is indication to the contrary, may apply the rule that a qualifying phrase qualifies only the word that is nearest to it. There is an instance in the first sentence in the preface to a former edition of this book: "For the assistance of students for the degree of Bachelor of Laws and articled clerks who were attending the tutorial classes conducted by solicitors." The articled clerks here referred to are clearly those who attend the classes. But are the students also those only who attend the classes? If we read on— "which the University of Melbourne arranged in 1941 as part of its course of study in law"—we may conclude that the students, also, were among those who attended the classes. But the client should not be left to anything so uncertain or so expensive as argument and decision of a court on the interpretation of the document.

An instance in a context where clarity is of great importance to all concerned is:

My trustees shall distribute my estate among institutions and societies and organisations whose purposes are charitable in the legal sense to be selected by them.

The organisations, it is clear, must be those whose purposes are charitable in the legal sense. But are the institutions and societies here included only those whose purposes are charitable in the legal sense?

The doubt may be avoided by such an arrangement as:

My trustees shall distribute my estate among such institutions, societies and organisations as they may select, provided that those they select are charitable.

This avoids also the awkwardness of placing "to be selected by them" after "sense" when it is intended to qualify "institutions and societies and organisations".

Sir Alison Russell[18] gives an example:

No pupil shall, on the ground of religious belief, be excluded from or placed in an inferior position in any school, college or hostel provided by the council.

As there may be doubt whether the phrase "provided by the council" refers only to "hostel" or whether it refers also to

18. Russell (1938), p 102. Although addressed to the drafter of statutes, it contains much advice useful in the work of a solicitor.

"school" and "college", the sentence may be re-arranged in either of the following ways, the first if the phrase refers only to "hostel":

No pupil shall, on the ground of religious belief, be excluded from or placed in an inferior position in any hostel provided by the council or in any school or college,

and if the phrase refers also to "school" and "college":

where a school, college or hostel is provided by the council no pupil shall, on the ground of religious belief, be excluded from or placed in an inferior position in the school, college or hostel.

Another example, where a comma after "at cost" might have helped to clarify a direction as to the method of valuing plant and equipment in order to ascertain the selling price of a company's shares on 30 April 1995:

Plant and equipment: **At the valuation appearing in the balance sheet as at 30 June 1994 plus additions and improvements at cost less depreciation calculated in accordance with the formula and at the rates applied in prior financial years for income tax purposes.**

Should the plant and equipment—in existence on 30 June 1994—be depreciated, or only the additions and improvements?

Judges have not agreed which words are modified by the phrase printed below in italics in a section of an early *Motor Car Act* of Victoria: [19]

10. (1) Every person who drives a motor car on a public highway recklessly or negligently or at a speed or in a manner which is dangerous to the public *having regard to all the circumstances of the case including the nature condition and use of the highway and to the amount of traffic which actually is at the time or which might reasonably be expected to be on the highway* **shall be guilty of an offence against this Act.**

In *Chammen v Gilmore*[20] it was held that the phrase modified all of the four preceding expressions, "recklessly", "negligently", "at a speed" and "in a manner"; in *Kane v Dureau*[21] it was treated as not applying to "recklessly".

19. Now repealed and replaced.
20. [1914] VLR 455.
21. [1911] VLR 293.

The following arrangements are clear:

A. If the phrase "having regard to . . . highway" is to apply to each of the four preceding expressions:

If a person drives a motor car on a public highway:
recklessly, or
negligently, or
at a speed which is dangerous to the public, or
in a manner which is dangerous to the public,
having regard to all the circumstances of the case, including the nature, condition and use of the highway, and to the amount of traffic which is actually at the time, or which might reasonably be expected to be, on the highway, he shall be guilty, etc.

Alternatively the phrase could be set out at length in the description of each offence.

B. If the phrase is to apply only to the last two of the expressions:

If a person drives a motor car on a public highway:
recklessly, or
negligently, or
at a speed or in a manner which is dangerous to the public, having regard in either case to all the circumstances . . . highway,
he shall be guilty, etc.

Thring in *Practical Legislation*[22] gives an instance of ambiguity in the use of the relative:

In a factory or workshop in which young children are employed.

The ambiguity here can be avoided by writing:

Where young children are employed in a factory or in a workshop,

or by repeating the antecedent as:

Every factory or workshop in which factory or workshop young children are employed.

The insertion of "in either event" prevents ambiguity in:

dies in my lifetime or dies after my death before attaining the age of 25 years and *in either event* leaves a child or children . . .

Other examples of syntactic ambiguity are discussed in later chapters.

22. Thring (1902), p 90.

5
Use of Definitions

This chapter discusses two sorts of definition:

(1) The use in a legal document of a descriptive word or phrase as a name or label for a party to a transaction or a person, date, thing or concept, which is to be referred to on a number of occasions; and

(2) a stipulative definition by which, for the purpose of a legal document, the ordinary meaning of a word is extended or limited or clarified.

The word "definition" is applied to the first use although it does not fall comfortably into the word's dictionary meaning: a statement or formal explanation of the meaning of a word or phrase.[1]

Use of descriptive word or phrase

When a name or description of a person, thing, event, or state of affairs first occurs in a document, it can be given a descriptive word or phrase for later reference. This can come immediately after the name or description, preferably in brackets; and introduced by the words *in this agreement* (or as the case may be) *called* " ", or simply *called* " ". The expression "hereinafter called" is often encountered. A method which has become common and which is economical is to place the word or phrase in brackets immediately after the expression it is to represent, as in:

The Northern Sand and Gravel Company Pty Ltd (Northern Sand).

The descriptive word or phrase is often in inverted commas in the definition, the inverted commas being omitted when the word or

---

1. Shorter Oxford English Dictionary—Clarendon Press (1993).

phrase is used later in the document. The use of inverted commas shows exactly what the descriptive word or phrase is: the "Trustee"; "the Trustee".

If a descriptive word used for a party is defined in a later clause so as to include persons besides the party referred to in the description—for instance, if the parties in question are trustees of a settlement, and later, in an interpretation clause, "Trustees" is defined to mean "the trustees for the time being of this settlement" the correct phrase to use after their names as parties to the deed is "in this deed *included* in the expression 'the Trustees' ".

Descriptive words or phrases can be usefully applied in many situations: to a date, a sum of money, a product, a ship, an invention; the list is endless. They can also be applied to elaborate concepts which may take many lines or pages to describe: "the moneys secured" by a mortgage debenture; the "net tangible assets" of a company or a group of companies.

Parties to a transaction

It is usual to give descriptive names to the parties to a transaction; it is convenient for the names to describe them in words appropriate to their connection with it. So a conveyance may commence with the words "This Conveyance is made the - 19 - between AB of etc (in this conveyance called 'the Vendor') of the one part and CD of etc (in this conveyance called 'the Purchaser') of the other part".

If one only of the parties is a company, it can be referred to as "the Company". This is not appropriate when two or more parties are companies. If there is no apt word to describe a person, then initials may be used: John William Smith (JWS); Elizabeth Jones Laboratories Pty Ltd (EJL); or a natural person's surname (McLeod) or an abbreviation of a corporate name. Repetition of the full name is thus avoided, also "the said" will not creep in.

Where there are provisions which are intended to affect *successors in title*, but in law will not do so unless the successors are mentioned, then, in order to avoid having to use words including them when they are mentioned in each of those provisions, the definition of a party can continue in the brackets:

(which expression where the context admits includes her successors in title).

Alternatively, an interpretation clause can provide that reference to a party shall, where the context admits, include reference to the party's successors in title or, if more suitable, executors, administrators and assigns or, in the case of a corporation, to its successors and assigns.

Reference to the successors in title, personal representatives or successors of a party may on many occasions be superfluous. In most Australian jurisdictions, the provisions of the *English Law of Property Act* 1925 have been adopted[2] and, by statute, a covenant relating to any land of the covenantee is deemed to be made with the covenantee and the covenantee's successors in title; and a covenant relating to any land of the covenantor is deemed to be made by the covenantor on behalf of the covenantor, her or his successors in title and the persons deriving title under him, her or them.

Pronouns in relation to descriptive words

Where a word, such as "Vendor" or "Mortgagor", has been used to refer to a party to an agreement, deed or other instrument, the party may consist of two or more persons. This situation arises particularly in the case of printed documents where each of the parties, in the eye of the author, is often a single male. Where it turns out that a party consists of several persons and it is necessary to add to the printed form one can say:

> "The Mortgagor warrant that they are the beneficial owners of the Mortgaged Property;"

or

> "The Mortgagor warrants that he is the beneficial owner of the Mortgaged Property."

Each of these sentences jars the reader. The first conveys the meaning more effectively.

Advantages of using definitions

Descriptive words or so called definitions by means of which a person or date or thing or concept is referred to by a descriptive word or phrase facilitate observance of the drafter's golden rule:

2. Vic: *Property Law Act* 1958, ss 78, 79.
   NSW: *Conveyancing Act* 1919, ss 70, 70A.

never change your language unless you wish to change your meaning. They also shorten documents. In Davidson's *Precedents*,[3] a covenant by the mortgagee with the mortgagor relating to the payment of the loan begins as follows:

> Provided also and the said [mortgagee] doth hereby for himself his heirs, executors and administrators covenant with said [mortgagor] his heirs, executors, administrators and assigns, that, if the said [mortgagor], his heirs, executors, administrators or assigns, shall . . .

This can be simplified by using a descriptive word for the parties and their personal representatives and successors:

> The mortgagee covenants with the mortgagor that if the mortgagor . . .

In a contract of sale of land, the drafter may find it necessary to refer on a number of occasions to "the date on which the purchaser becomes entitled to possession of the land sold or to receipt of the rents and profits". Instead of repeating this phrase on each occasion, it can be defined the first time it is used by the addition after it of words such as: ("the Completion Date"). Thereafter these three words can be used instead of the 22 words of the original phrase.

Stipulative definitions

A stipulative definition can ascribe a meaning to a word where the dictionary sense is not clear or which needs to be made more precise or it can extend or restrict a word's dictionary meaning.

Where a word is to be used in its everyday or dictionary meaning, a definition should not need to be set out in a document unless the word has two senses which may be confused:

"month" means calendar month.

A word or expression may be defined by using the verb *means*, as: " 'Directors' means the directors of the Company for the time being"; a statement whose import is that "Directors" *means only* or *has no other meaning than* "the directors of the Company for the time being".

3. Davidson (1881), Vol II, Pt II, pp 884-886.

"Includes" may be used to enlarge the natural meaning or a stipulated meaning, or to clarify it:

"literary work" includes a written table or compilation.

"spouse" includes a de facto spouse.

The Victorian *Property Law Act* 1958, s 18(1) provides that " 'Notice' includes constructive notice", that is "notice" has among its meaning "constructive notice" but has, or may have, other meanings (actual notice). "Includes" applied to a word imports "first what it would ordinarily mean and also something else which it does not ordinarily mean, but which, for convenience, is declared to be included in it".[4]

"Motor Car" includes a motor cycle.

Where the concepts expressed to be included in the definition may colour the ordinary meaning of a defined word, the expression "but is not limited to" may be used:

"Mortgage" includes, but is not limited to, a charge or lien on real or personal property to secure money.

If a list of concepts forms part of the definition, care must be taken that the meaning attributed to the defined term is not limited through being restricted to the concepts listed or to items of the same sort as the listed concepts. The expressed concepts may colour the meaning of the defined term. The expressions "but is not limited to" or "without limiting the foregoing" will help to negate this restriction. For further discussion of this topic, see below, p 110.

The expression "but does not include" or "excludes" may be used to restrict the natural meaning or a stipulated meaning or, again, to clarify it. The following example is taken from s 9 of the Corporations Law:

" 'emoluments' means the amount or value of any money, consideration or benefit given, directly or indirectly, to a director of a body corporate in connection with the management of the affairs of the body or of any holding company or subsidiary of the body, whether as a director or otherwise, but does not include amounts in payment or reimbursement of out-of-pocket expenses incurred for the benefit of the body."

"The expression *means and includes* should never be used, since these words have different significations."[5] But there is often a

---

4. Russell (1938), p 40.

temptation to use both. In the articles of association of a company "Directors" has been defined in the words:

"Directors" means the directors for the time being of the Company.

and the word has been used in a number of articles and refers to directors who are elected by the shareholders. Provision then has to be made for alternate directors who are to be appointed by the elected directors and are to act for them in their absence. The definition of "Directors" is altered to read:

"Directors" means the directors for the time being of the Company and includes alternate directors appointed under article -.

This definition is not satisfactory. For instance, if one third of directors retire each year and there are six directors and each has appointed an alternate director, then, in accordance with the definition, four directors will retire each year, instead of two as was probably intended.

It is difficult to find an effective definition of Directors which includes alternates. A solution, in this particular case, is to leave unaltered the original definition ("Directors means the directors for the time being of the Company") and to provide that an alternate, in the absence of the principal, is to be counted as a director and may exercise all the powers of the principal.

Both "means" and "includes" (but not the two together) are used in the definition of "fishing operations" in s 6 of the *Income Tax Assessment Act* (Cth):

"fishing operations" means:

(a) operations relating directly to the catching of fish, turtles, dugong, crustacea or oysters or other shellfish; or

(b) pearling operations,

and includes oyster farming, but does not include whaling, and also does not include operations conducted otherwise than for the purpose of business.

It is sometimes convenient to import a statutory definition by reference. This may be because it is required that, in the document, the defined term should have the same meaning as it has in the statute; or because the statutory definition is long and it would be economical of space not to have it set out at length. The disadvantage is that the reader must go to the statute for the definition. The document's audience may be familiar with it.

"Subsidiary" means a body corporate which is a subsidiary of XY Ltd within the meaning of division 6 of part 1.2 of the Corporations Law as from time to time in force.

Misuse of definitions

Substantive provisions should not be placed in an interpretation clause. The definition "Completion Date means 30 June 1995 on which date the Purchaser is obliged to pay the residue of purchase money" is undesirable. The obligation to pay the residue of purchase money should be in the section of the document which deals with that element of the transaction. If the obligation is mentioned in the definition there may be doubt whether it is intended to create a legal obligation in that context.

Dickerson[5] draws attention to the danger, when using stipulative definitions, of giving a term a meaning which differs significantly from the sense in which it is ordinarily understood. The reader may find it difficult to adapt to the strained language and even the drafter may become confused.

Capital initial letters

Defined terms can be distinguished in the text of a document by the use of a different type such as italics or by being printed wholly in capitals. It is not difficult to achieve these distinctions with modern equipment. The usual method is by spelling the defined term with an initial capital letter. If the defined term consists of several words, the first word may be spelt with an initial capital or all words, other than articles, prepositions, pronouns and conjunctions, may be spelt with initial capitals.

Thus, if a party to a document is a company, it can be referred to throughout as "the Company", leaving "company" without a capital for use if a company in general is meant. The device of using a capital letter is particularly helpful when, as in this instance, the descriptive word is likely to be used also in a different sense. Use

5. Dickerson (1965), Ch 7.

of the capital letter brings to the reader's attention that for the purpose of the document a particular meaning has been given to the word.

The drafter should be aware whether or not the defined term includes the article. If "the Cargo" is defined and the drafter writes "Cargo" without the article, intending to use the defined term, the intention may not be clear to the reader, or to a court.

"And" or "or" in definitions

The authorities on parliamentary drafting allow the use either of "and" or of "or" in a definition in which the expression defined may apply to several objects. For instance:

> **"bullock" includes any cow, bullock and ox,**
> **"bullock" includes any cow, bullock or ox.**

But Russell[6] suggests that:

> Where the intention is that the things mentioned are to be separate, it is advisable always to use "or", since this course prevents any doubt arising, even though the doubt be momentary and ocular.

> For example:

> **"trading" means buying and selling.**
> **"trading" includes buying and selling.**

> In the above case a doubt might arise whether "buying" alone or "selling" alone constitutes trading.

> Where the intention is that the things mentioned are not to be separate, this should be made clear.

> For example:

> **"trading" means buying and selling, but not buying alone or selling alone.**

If the things mentioned are set out in paragraphs, the use of a connective can be avoided; as in:

> **"associated company" means any of the following:**
> **a company in which the Company holds shares;**
> **a company which holds shares in the Company;**
> **a company which is controlled by persons who control the Company.**

6. Russell (1938), p 42.

Expression used in two meanings

If it is convenient to use an expression in two slightly different but connected meanings, the definition may use the phrase "as circumstances require", as in:

"Agreement" means, as circumstances require, the agreement between the parties whereby their differences have been settled or the document in which that agreement is recorded.

Definitions diminish errors in completing a draft

Suppose a date—for instance the commencing date of the arrangements provided for in an agreement—occurs many times in the document. When the first draft is made, the commencing date is to be 2 April. Later it is found that it will be 18 April. It is then necessary to alter the date whenever it occurs. This takes up valuable time and it may be that every date will not be altered. This can be avoided if, in place of the date, the expression "the Commencing Date" is used, and in the interpretation clause the commencing date is defined in the words "the Commencing Date means   ", or, which may be more flexible, "the Commencing Date means   or such other date as the parties may agree upon in writing." This blank alone is left to be completed when the document is ready to be executed.

Interpretation clause

If there are many words or phrases to be defined they can be collected in an interpretation clause, as is done in an Act of Parliament. But if a definition is needed only in one operative clause, it may be clearer to put it in that clause and not in the general interpretation clause.

An interpretation clause is best placed at the beginning of a document which can then be read with the definitions in mind. It is commonly introduced by such an expression as:

In this [document], unless a contrary intention appears

or

In this [document], unless inconsistent with the context or subject matter

or

In this [document], where the context so admits

Such a formula is a safeguard against the error that would result from an unqualified definition if a defined word were inadvertently, but obviously, used in a sense other than the one defined. Such a use may readily occur if the word is one in common use, for instance if a company party to a document is defined as "the Company", and afterwards there is mention of another company and that company happens to be referred to as "the Company". Care in drafting would avoid this; but it is difficult in a long document to be quite certain no such mistake has been made, particularly if the original draft has to be substantially revised.

The use in an interpretation clause of such a formula as "unless the context otherwise requires" has been criticised "as saying no more than 'X *may* mean Y' ".[7] It has been described as an abdication of responsibility and "inexcusable in these days of word processors and computers which allow us to check easily every occurrence of a word in a text".[8] However, whether or not the formula is included, a court would almost certainly apply it in construing a document.[9]

The drafter should make quite clear whether the terms defined in the interpretation clause are to be used with a capital or small initial letter.

Cognate words

When a word has been defined, and other expressions derived from it are also to be used, it is not necessary to have a definition for each. For instance, in the *Copyright Act* 1968 (Cth), s 10:

"writing" means a mode of representing words in a visible form and "written" *has a corresponding meaning.*

Another mode of expression is used in:

"abet" *with its grammatical variations and cognate expressions* **has the same meaning as in the Penal Code (Russell).**

7. Dickerson (1965), p 70.
8. Victorian Law Reform Commission, Discussion Paper No 1, p 29.
9. *Meux v Jacobs* (1875) LR 7 HL 481 at 493.

Statutory definitions

In most jurisdictions the English *Law of Property Act* 1925 has been copied, and accordingly there are some statutory definitions which render similar definitions in various documents unnecessary. In Victoria, by legislation now found in the *Property Law Act* 1958, s 61:

> "In all deeds, contracts, wills, orders and other instruments executed, made or coming into operation after the commencement of the Act, unless the context otherwise requires:
> (a) 'Month' means calender month;
> (b) 'Person' includes a corporation;
> (c) The singular includes the plural, and *vice versa*;
> (d) The masculine includes the feminine, and *vice versa*."

Drafting

When preparing the first draft of a long document, the drafter will be helped by having a list of defined terms. Melville[10] recommends that definitions be set out on a separate sheet. The definitions can then be referred to while drawing the document and can be readily altered or added to.

Successive drafts of a document should be denoted so that they can be identified. The date of a draft can be noted on it and the initials of the person who prepared it. It is sometimes important that successive drafts can be identified by date and placed in chronological order.

---

10. Melville (1985), p 11.

6
Language

The length and prolixity of early legal documents was mentioned above in Chapter 1. This chapter discusses the avoidance of some bad drafting habits which still persist but which are now less prevalent and also discusses several topics relating to language generally. Particular words and constructions are discussed in later chapters.

Verbosity

In many of the older forms, two words, sometimes more, are used to express varieties of ways of thinking of what might be expressed by a single word. "Lands tenements and hereditaments" was formerly used—and there may have been a time when each word was necessary—for what may now be called "land" or "property". "Tenements" is obsolete and "hereditaments" referred to property which descended to an heir and, generally speaking, is not now a suitable word, the status of heir no longer being significant in Australian legal systems.

"Covenants conditions agreements or stipulations" is used in: "If the tenant at any time makes default in or neglects or fails to perform or observe or fulfil any of the covenants conditions agreements or stipulations herein contained or implied and which on the part of the tenant are or ought to be performed observed or fulfilled." If these four words are needed to describe the provisions which impose obligations on the tenant, the passage can be recast: "If the tenant fails to perform or observe an obligation on his [her] part." If "covenant" is sufficient, it can be used instead of "obligation" or the passage may be reworded: "If the tenant commits a breach of any of the tenant's covenants." The author is trying to be comprehensive by describing exhaustively the provisions of the lease that may impose an obligation on the tenant. If the lease is a deed, those provisions will fall within the description of "covenant", a word meaning technically a promise under seal. However, the drafter does have a problem. If in one clause the tenant is expressed to *covenant* with the landlord and, in another, to *agree* with the landlord, to do or not to do certain things, and the passage is reworded: "If there is a breach of any of the tenant's covenants . . .", the tenant will argue that, in the context of the lease, this passage applies only to obligations which the tenant expressly *covenanted* to carry out, not to those which he expressly *agreed* to do. The better course is to refer to "obligations" rather than to "covenants".

In a lease, the tenant covenants well and sufficiently to repair, uphold and maintain the leased premises. In *Calthorpe v McOscar*[1] it was doubted whether the additional words added anything to the meaning of the word "repair".

The expression "all the mortgagor's interest in the chattels", could, if there was a definition of "chattels", take the place of "all the right title interest property benefit claim and demand whatsoever of the mortgagor in to upon or in respect of the several chattels effects matters and things hereby assigned or herein comprised and every or any of them respectively".

The verbose style of drafting of which the last quoted phrase is a surpassing example has gone out of fashion over the last four or five decades. One now seldom sees documents in which the names of the parties are followed by a recurring "his (her or their) executors administrators and assigns". The addition of these words is usually unnecessary and, if it is necessary, its recurrence can be avoided as explained earlier.[2] Nor is the formula "person or persons corporation or corporations" required today to embrace the totality of legal entities. The adoption in Australian jurisdictions of s 61 of the *English Property Law Act* 1925 makes "person" sufficient in place of the six words quoted.

The former use in conveyances of a great number of words to express the transfer of the estate or interest—now replaced by a single word—has already been mentioned.[3] "This multiplication of useless expressions", wrote Davidson in 1860,[4] "probably

---

1. [1924] 1 KB 716.
2. See above, pp 43-44.
3. See above, pp 7-8.
4. Davidson (1860), Vol 1, p 67.

owed its origin to the want of knowledge of the true meaning and due application of each word, and a consequent apprehension that, if one word alone were used, a wrong one might be adopted and the right one omitted; and to this something must be added for carelessness and the general disposition of the profession to seek safety in verbosity rather than in discrimination of language''.

Avoidance of antique words and expressions not used in ordinary affairs

Of these the most frequently occurring are *the said* and its synonym *the aforesaid*. If any person or thing is mentioned it used to be the custom, whenever the name or description occurred again, to preface it by the words ''the said'' or ''the aforesaid''. Common sense suggests that, if a person is referred to in a document by name, a subsequent mention of that name, unqualified by ''said'' or ''aforesaid'', will be understood as referring to that person, unless a contrary intention appears.[5] Nevertheless, ''said'' still appears in legal documents. It is true that if several different persons or things are mentioned it may, in most unusual cases, as where two persons have exactly the same name, be necessary to distinguish them, and sometimes a convenient way to do this is to use one of these expressions. There is another way—the use of a definition[6]—which does away with the use of ''said'' and ''aforesaid''.

But there are many documents in which it is absurd to pretend to distinguish a person or thing when no confusion is possible. For instance, if a husband appoints as an executrix of his will ''my wife A'', it is mere irritation to the reader to call her, whenever she is named later in the will, ''my said wife A''; for ''my wife A'' can refer to no other person than the wife already named. Or if a date, say, 15 April 1994, has to be mentioned again, it is ridiculous to write ''the said 15 April 1994''.

Conveyances, and other documents, may contain a series of recitals, each introduced by *whereas*. The use of this word in conveyances is traditional but not necessary. It is possible to avoid its repetition. One way of doing it is to put all the recitals into a schedule where they can be set out less formally and with no

5. Parker (1964), p 6.
6. See above, Chapter 5.

"whereas" and to state that the document is entered into having regard to the matters recited in the schedule. If, as often happens, the recitals need to be read so as to enable the document to be understood, they are more conveniently placed at the beginning than in a schedule. An introductory "whereas" may be used, followed by numbered or lettered paragraphs. Another way is to introduce them with "Recitals" and so obviate the use of "whereas".

So also hereinbefore, hereinafter, hereafter, thereof, thereto, and the many similar referential words, should not be used except where they are clearly the best words. They have the added disadvantage that they are popularly regarded as legal jargon and may be criticised on this account. At times they may be apt and may achieve brevity as against the alternative which would usually be a circumlocution. Although, carefully used, these words are an aid to exact expression, some of them are affected with uncertainty. There are occasions when it may not be clear whether *herein* means "in this document" or "in this present clause"; in such a case one of these expressions should be used rather than "herein".

The same is a favourite expression of drafters. "I devise my farming lands to my trustees upon trust to sell the same." Anyone outside a lawyer's office would say "upon trust to sell them", and there could be no doubt of the meaning. In most places where we use "the same" a pronoun would do, or it would be natural to repeat the word or words. But there are contexts where the expression "the same" is exactly what is required, being short and definite and avoiding repetition.

Since the first edition of this book was published, some of the examples of redundancy have become less common, even rare, as a result of the more enlightened approach to drafting that has developed.

A party was often said to "covenant and agree". Either verb alone is sufficient. "Covenant" should, strictly, be confined to deeds. Covenants sometimes used to be in the form "shall and will" or "shall not nor will". Use of both auxiliaries is pointless.

A person might be required to "pay and discharge" [or to "bear pay satisfy and discharge"] rates, taxes and charges on land. To pay them would be enough. Debts were described as being or becoming "due and payable". In most cases, there is no distinction between the two words.

Fourteen days "shall be and are hereby fixed". It is more economical to say: "are fixed".

"By and in the said deed of settlement declared and contained" can be replaced with "contained in the settlement".

In a will, an asset which was subject to a life interest might be said, on the death of the life tenant, to "fall into and become part of my residuary estate". Either "fall into" or "become part of" would be adequate.

"All and singular the furniture" means no more than "all the furniture" or "the furniture".

"This is my last will" says as much as "This is my last will and testament."

Instead of "It shall be lawful for any of the assignees . . ." or "It shall not be lawful for any of the assignees . . .", the same effect will be attained in most documents by "An assignee may . . ." or "An assignee may not . . .".

It is hardly necessary to say that there is no need to keep the antique form in "th" for the third person singular, or constructions with "do" that are not now in ordinary use. "Hath agreed", "do hereby grant", can be written "has agreed", "hereby grant" or "grant". "AB Ltd doth hereby give notice" should be rejected in favour of "AB Ltd gives notice". In spite of the common practice of using the word "witnesseth" in deeds, the word "witnesses" is just as effective. "Situate", meaning situated, is often encountered; the more modern "situated" is to be preferred.

Pronouns

Repetition of the same phrases or descriptions is, if possible, to be avoided because it makes the document tedious to the reader. A method of avoiding repetition is by the use of a pronoun, but only if there is no lack of clarity. It is better to be inelegant than uncertain. In the following sentence, the use of "she" or "her" for either "tenant" or "landlord", in any place where either word occurs, would make the meaning unclear:

If the Tenant fails to perform any obligation on her part contained in this lease, the Landlord may make good the default at the expense of the Tenant; the full amount of the expenses incurred by the Landlord in so doing together with

interest on that amount at the rate of 12 per cent per annum computed from the date of payment of those expenses by the Landlord shall be paid by the Tenant to the Landlord on demand.

Ambiguity and lack of clarity must be avoided when pronouns are used. Repetition is better than the slightest chance of ambiguity.

Restraint in use of "such"

"Such" is a word that can cause ambiguity. Some authorities think its use as a demonstrative undesirable when referring to something that has already been mentioned:[7]

> **"The word 'such' is not infrequently used in Acts when the word 'the' or 'that' would be more correct. In the first place 'the' or 'that' is better English; and, in the next place, the general use of the word 'such' may cause confusion to arise when it is desired to use the word 'such' in its correct meaning."**[8]

What is here referred to as the correct meaning is "such" followed by "as"; simple cases are "in such manner as", "such charges as are mentioned in this deed".

The objections to the use of "such" as a demonstrative for a previous noun are that sometimes it may not be certain which of several nouns is referred to, or, if the noun is certain, whether any phrases that qualify it are implied by the reference; and sometimes the reader may not think back to what has already been mentioned but may be looking for a correlative "as" to follow and show what the "such" refers to.

The latter difficulty may be resolved on a careful reading or re-reading of the sentence, but the reader should not be required to concentrate unduly on material which could have been expressed simply. The following passage illustrates that the use of "such" can be confusing:

7. Sir Frederick Pollock, while editor of the Law Reports, wrote to Justice Oliver Wendell Holmes of the Supreme Court of the United States: "As to *such*, this is the kind of attorney's clerk's slang I have tried to choke off: 'The plaintiff was the tenant of a house in X street. Such street was admitted to be a new street within etc, etc.' They think it looks more professional. And so it has crept even into judgments." *Pollock-Holmes Letters*, Vol II, p 251.
8. Russell (1938), p 87.

If, in respect of the sublicence for the use of the patent, an additional royalty becomes payable by the sublicensor in consequence of an improvement in any of the inventions protected by such patent, the sublicensee shall pay such additional royalty in respect of such inventions in which such improvement has been made as the sublicensor specifies.

It is not clear whether the final words, "as the sublicensor specifies," relate back to "such additional royalty" or to "such inventions."

The construction "such . . . as" can often be avoided. The expression "the charges mentioned in this deed" means the same as "such charges as are mentioned in this deed" and "Upon trust for such of his children as are alive at or born after my death" can be put more briefly "upon trust for his children who are alive at or born after my death".

The construction is, however, useful for linking a noun with a qualifying clause from which it is separated:

The sublicensee shall pay such additional royalty in respect of the invention to which the improvement has been made as is agreed upon by the parties or, failing agreement, as is determined in accordance with clause—.

Another objection to "such" as a demonstrative attached to a noun that has already been mentioned appears when a qualifying phrase is attached to the noun. The doubt is then whether the noun when mentioned in the second place is qualified by the phrase attached to it in the first place.

In *Mountifield v Ward*,[9] a Divisional Court considered s 10 of the English *Licensing Act* 1874:

"10. Nothing in this Act or in the principal Act contained shall preclude a person licensed to sell any intoxicating liquor to be consumed on the premises from selling *such liquor* **at any time to bona fide travellers."**

Did this section permit the sale of intoxicating liquor to bona fide travellers for consumption only on the premises or did it permit sale for consumption off the premises? Wright and Bruce JJ decided that the intention of the section was such that the former was the correct construction, that is, the words "such liquor" referred not

9. [1897] 1 QB 326. See also *Re Hodgkinson* (1947) 75 CLR 276.

only to "intoxicating liquor" but to "intoxicating liquor to be consumed on the premises". The ambiguity of the phrase is emphasised by the fact that the decision rested on the apparent intention and not on the precise construction of the words used.

It is difficult to construe the following subclause sometimes found in the "objects" clause of a company's memorandum of association and derived from earlier editions of Palmer's *Precedents*:

> **To lend money to such persons or companies and on such terms as may seem expedient, and in particular to customers and others having dealings with the Company, and to guarantee the performance of contracts by any such persons or companies.**

The Company's power to guarantee the performance of contracts appears to be restricted to those of persons or companies to whom it has lent money.

Technical terms

A solicitor who is drafting in plain English may find that technical terms are needed, especially where the technical term could not be expressed in non-technical language except at some length. Plain English does not exclude technical terms.

Technical terms have evolved in the practice of the law. Other professions, and businesses, have their own technical terms.

Lawyers have developed words and phrases which have a specific and precise meaning:

> **Some expressions in common use in legal documents dealing with legal rights or obligations acquire in a legal context a special meaning different from, or more precise than, their meaning in common speech—they become "terms of art".** [10]

Not to use a technical term in its proper place would be an affectation as noticeable as the over-frequent use of such words when they are not needed. For instance, in a will, the terms "residue" and "testamentary expenses" would be understood as terms of art by those practising in the field. A non-lawyer, while having a general notion of their meaning, might not know their exact signification.

---

10. *Prestcold (Central) Ltd v Minister of Labour* [1969] 1 All ER 69 at 75, per Lord Diplock.

Terms of art are sometimes referred to disparagingly as "legal jargon" but those which serve a valuable purpose should be distinguished from other legal jargon which serves no such purpose and should be abandoned.

In commercial documents the ordinary phraseology of business should be used although it may not be the everyday language of people not engaged in business. Parties who buy and sell goods which are to be transported to the buyer by ship, would be familiar with the expressions cif and fob, and would be able to mention them in their dealings without explanation.

Terms which have a technical meaning in a profession should be used in the strict sense in which they are understood in that profession. A "receipts and payments" account, a summarised statement of actual cash receipts and cash payments over a period, should be used in the sense in which it is understood by accountants and should not be confused with an "income and expenditure account," a summarised statement of the income earned and the expenditure incurred during the period.

In the preparation of documents relating to real property, it will be best to use the technical terms that are appropriate to the dealing. If the appearance of over-legality is to be avoided, it must be by devices of arrangement and by the omission of "whereas," "aforesaid," "hereinafter" and other legal jargon.

Words of similar sound

Words such as "employer" and "employee" can be confused, particularly when dictating. The document will be easier to read and there will be less chance of error if they are replaced by such words as "company" and "manager" or as "employer" and "engineer". Instead of "lessor" and "lessee", "landlord" and "tenant" can be used and for "mortgagor" and "mortgagee", "borrower" and "lender".

Choice may be restricted in the case of Torrens system forms, in which the expressions "mortgagor" and "mortgagee", "lessor" and "lessee" are prescribed.

"Not" and "now" are surprisingly often mistaken for each other. The substitution of one for the other may reverse the intended meaning of a sentence. A letter to a mortgagee who is prepared to release the security without receiving repayment of the loan in full: "The outstanding balance of the loan will not be secured" has a very different message from: "The outstanding balance of the loan will now be secured."

Gender neutral language

People engaged in drafting will find, more and more, that they will be required to prepare documents in gender neutral language,[11] particularly those which are of wide or general application such as the constitution of a club or society, the articles of association of a public company, documents connected with consumer transactions. This conforms with the style now adopted for legislation.

Words which imply a gender, or appear to do so, such as chairman, draftsman, matron, policeman, can be replaced with gender neutral words such as chairperson or chair, drafter, director of nursing, police officer. Some words such as testator, executor, author, which have a feminine form but which do not blatantly refer to the male sex, seem to be acceptable as having become words that apply to both sexes.

Third person singular pronouns, he, she and their derivatives, him, her, his, hers, are not gender neutral, unlike other pronouns, including the relative pronouns, who, whom and whose. The definite and indefinite articles are gender neutral.

Where a third person singular pronoun might have been used, the sentence can be amended or restructured to make it gender neutral.

The double pronoun (he or she) can be used or the gender specific pronoun can be replaced by the noun which it represents. Regulation 95(1) of the uniform Companies Codes of the 1980s is shown with amendments which bring about gender neutrality:

> **A notice may be given by the company to any member either by serving it on him [him or her] [the member] personally or by sending it by post to him [him or her] [the member] at his [his or her] [the member's] address as shown in the register of members or the address supplied by him [him or her] [the member] to the company for the giving of notices to him [him or her] [the member].**

11. On gender neutral language, see Victorian Law Reform Commission, *Drafting Manual*, pp 58-59, paras 127-128; Kimble, pp 85-86.

Combining the two methods would produce the best result.

While clarity takes precedence over elegance, tedium should be avoided if practicable. Too much reliance on double pronouns or repeated nouns can make the sentence cumbersome.

A sentence can sometimes be put in the plural without affecting the meaning. Plural pronouns cover all genders. In the last example, putting "notice", "member" and "address" in the plural produces an unclear regulation even with some other amendments. However:

A drafter should aim to make his work intelligible.

becomes

Drafters should aim to make their work intelligible.

The third person singular pronoun can sometimes be replaced with "the" "a" or "an" or deleted altogether:

In the case of an equality of votes, the chairperson has a casting vote, in addition to his [a] deliberative vote.

A committee member who is absent from three successive meetings shall vacate [his] office.

The sentence can be put into the passive voice:

Before:

When the draftsman foresees doubt whether his "and" will be read in the conjunctive sense, or in the disjunctive sense of "or", he should make his meaning clear.

After:

When doubt is foreseen whether "and" will be read in the conjunctive sense, or in the disjunctive sense of "or", the meaning should be made clear.

The sentence can be recast by deleting surplus words or in other ways so that it applies to both sexes.

If a partner attains the age of 68 years, he shall retire from the partnership on the next 30 June.

becomes:

A partner who attains the age of 68 years shall retire from the partnership on the next 30 June.

In some documents, consumer contracts, for example, the supplier of goods or services who proffers the document, can be described as "we" and the other party can be described as "you". "We" and "you" are gender neutral.

7
"Shall"

"Shall" in stating cases, occasions and conditions

Formerly it was the general practice, and it is still not unusual, to use the verbal form "shall" not only in declaring the will or agreement of the parties as to what shall or shall not be done in the future on a stated occasion or in stated circumstances or subject to a stated condition, but also in defining the occasions or circumstances or conditions. This was the practice in statutes also.

Coode discusses this practice in the drafting of statutes.[1]

"The attempt to express every action referred to in a statute in a future tense renders the language complicate, anomalous, and difficult to be understood. The practice is founded apparently on a false assumption that the words '*shall*' and '*shall not*' put the enacting verb into the future tense. But in all commanding language at least the word 'shall' is modal, not temporal; it denotes the compulsion, the obligation to act (*scealan*, to owe, to be obliged), and does not prophesy that the party will or will not at some future time do the act. 'Thou shalt do no murder' is not a prediction, but the 'shalt' is obligatory in the present tense, continuously through all the time of the operation of the law."

Coode deplores that clauses, such as cases[2] and conditions, that are subordinate to the imperative or commanding clause, have been put into the future tense, either because of the influence of "shall" in the imperative clause (the legal action) or fear that the provision will be held to apply only to the circumstances existing when it came into force. Coode points out that this fear is unfounded. The

1. Coode (1843), pp xxvii, xxviii.
2. For *case* and *condition*, see above, pp 31-33.

law must be regarded while it remains in force as constantly speaking. The same continuous operation will apply to private legal documents. This rule in the constitution of a society is not restricted to committee members who held office when the rule came into force:

> **A committee member who has served on the committee for a continuous period of seven years shall not be eligible for re-election at the annual general meeting next following the expiration of that period.**

In clauses subordinate to the legal action, it is preferable to use the present tense to set out facts which are to be concurrent with the legal action and the perfect tense for facts required to have preceded the legal action.

A simple example of the change from "shall" to the present in stating a condition:

> **If the purchaser *shall fail* to pay when due any instalment of principal or interest, the whole of the principal with interest to date of payment shall immediately become payable.**

This becomes:

> **If the purchaser *fails* to pay when due any instalment of principal or interest, the whole of the principal with interest to date of payment shall immediately become payable.**

Another example:

> **If A *shall have made* default in the performance of this covenant, etc, and if B *shall* serve notice on him of the default, and the default *shall* continue for 14 days, B shall upon the expiration of that period of default be entitled, etc.**

This becomes:

> **If at any time A *has made* default in the performance of this covenant, etc, and B *serves* notice on him of the default, and the default *continues* for 14 days, B shall be entitled [or may] upon the expiration of that period of default, etc.**

The use of the present or the perfect tense for subordinate clauses, instead of the future tense, has two advantages:

(1) It avoids the need for complicated grammatical constructions in subordinate clauses often involving the use of the future and future perfect:

> **if a person *shall* be convicted of, etc, and if he *shall have been* before convicted of the same offence; and if he *shall* not *have* undergone the punishment which he should have undergone for the offence of which he *shall have been* so before convicted .**

(2) By keeping the description of *cases* and *conditions* in the present and perfect tenses, the imperative language of the *legal action* may be clearly distinguished from the language of the subordinate clauses. Narration will appear in narrative language, instead of being allowed to usurp imperious language.

In modern statutes it is invariably assumed that they are "constantly speaking" and so the present indicative or present perfect tense is adopted, the word "shall" being used as an imperative only, and not as a future.[3]

In the Victorian consolidation of 1915 what was there described as "the modern practice" of confining the words "shall" and "may" and "shall not" and "may not" to cases where the legislature is issuing a command or granting or negating a power was observed. As "really a mild example" of the improvement in expression that resulted, the Explanatory Paper in the first volume gives the following:

> **"In the *Railways Act* 1890, s 6 provided: 'where any goods shall be delivered to be carried along or upon any railway, and the same shall have been carried safely to the place to which the Commissioners . . . shall have undertaken to carry the same, and shall have been duly discharged from the truck in which they were carried, the said Commissioners . . . shall be responsible only as bailees for custody . . . until the removal of the same by the consignee thereof.'**

> **In the *Railways Act* 1915, s 6 reads: 'Where any goods delivered to be carried along or upon any railway have been carried safely to the place to which the Commissioners . . . have undertaken to carry them, and have been duly discharged from the truck in which they have been carried, the Commissioners . . . shall until the removal of such goods by the consignees thereof be responsible only as bailees for custody, etc.' "**

3. Compare Thring (1902), p 83.

As the Victorian Full Court said in *Attorney-General v Craig*:[4]

"there is an increasing tendency in the drafting of modern statutes to use the present tense to express provisions intended to operate continuously upon transactions or events which will occur after the provisions come into force."

What Coode says of the objections to "shall" in statutes applies to business documents.

There may be doubts whether the courts would hold that a document between parties in which cases, occasions, circumstances, conditions and the like were expressed in the present or perfect and not in the future should be interpreted as applying whenever (within the words of the document) the case, occasion or circumstance arose or the condition had to be satisfied. Although a general formal statement to this effect may not be found in the reports there can be no doubt that this is correct. If in a particular clause there seems any room for doubt whether a statement in the present tense will be so interpreted, the doubt can usually be avoided by introducing it with some such phrase as *if at any time.*

The way is therefore open for restricting the use of "shall" to the expression of the will of the parties concerning future actions in pursuance of the document. If this practice is followed, the language will be less cumbersome. They may also avoid positive errors, such as have resulted from the use of "shall" in a will, a document written now but to take effect in the future.

There have been many applications to the courts to decide whether or not such language as:

In case any child of mine shall die in my lifetime leaving children living at my death those children shall stand in place of the deceased child.[5]

included the children of a child who was dead at the date of the will. Such words must, prima facie, be given their proper grammatical meaning, with the result (often quite contrary to what one would expect a testator to intend), that children of a child who died before the date of the will are excluded.[6] The context may show that the intention of the testator was otherwise and the courts have at times been able to find the contrary intention in

4. [1958] VR 34 at 38.
5. See (1936) 9 ALJ 326 at 327.
6. *Re Cope* [1908] 2 Ch 1; *Re Walker* [1930] 1 Ch 469.

the language of the will itself.[7] However, in *Re McPherson*,[8] the passage "if any of my children . . . shall predecease me leaving children him or her surviving . . ." was held to have in the context its literal meaning and the children of a child of the testator who died before the date of the will were excluded.

It is a useful general rule that, in a will, if a condition is stated that either may have already been performed at the date of the will, or may be performed after that date, the words used should cover both possibilities. Where a child has died before the will is made, leaving children, if those children, the testator's grandchildren, are to take the deceased child's share, the testator can use the present tense instead of the future, and also use some such wording as: "if any child of mine dies before me, whether before or after the execution of this will, leaving children . . .".

In another case, a sum of money was given by will to trustees "to be held upon trust and disposed of by them among such person, persons or charities *as may be notified by me* to them during my lifetime". These words were held to exclude a trust notified by the testator before the date of the will.[9] (In that particular instance the clause would have been invalid even if the language used had included anterior notifications as well as future notifications.)[10] It will, in general, be sufficient to state that the condition may have been or may be satisfied "before or after the execution of this will", if that is the testator's intention. The drafter's duty is to prevent any occasion for doubt.

If it is agreed that cases and conditions are to be stated in the present and the perfect, the next question is—in what mood? Coode considered that the case should be in the subjunctive, but that "as subjunctive language cannot be distinguished from conditional, and as conditional language is more specifically necessary for the expression of *the condition*, it would appear to be better, in describing the case, to use the still more ordinary language of the indicative mood". His advice then is to state the case in the indicative and the condition in the conditional—"if he insist", "if it appear", "if the court order".

7. *Loring v Thomas* (1861) 1 Dr & Sm 497; 62 ER 469; *Re Lambert* [1908] 2 Ch 117; *Re Birchall* [1940] Ch 424. In *Re Anderson* [1927] VLR 279.
8. [1968] VR 368.
9. *Re Keen; Evershed v Griffiths* [1937] Ch 236.
10. Ibid at 246.

Since Coode's day, the conditional in this form (which is the same as the subjunctive) has been gradually going out of use. The alternative forms "if he should insist", "if it should appear", "if the court should order" would now be used when a conditional form of expression was necessary. But in conditions also, as in cases, the indicative has become the usual form of expression.

Where the contributions payable by a member have been reduced, if the trustees are satisfied that . . . , they may . . .

Unnecessary use of "shall"

Substitution of the present or perfect indicative in subordinate clauses for "shall" has been mentioned. There are other occasions on which it is better not to use it. In an interpretation clause, it is sufficient to say: " 'Seal' *means* the common seal of the company," rather than "*shall mean*". "The general conditions in the third schedule to the *Property Law Act* 1958 *apply* to this contract", instead of "*shall apply*".

Where the obligation is created by the opening words of an instrument, or a clause, it is unnecessary and inelegant to repeat words of obligation in passages governed by those opening words.

The Tenant covenants with the Landlord:
That the tenant will (rather than "shall" or "must") keep the leased premises in repair.

The parties agree that each of them will pay an equal proportion of the stamp duty on this deed.

The opening sentence of condition 1 of Table A in the seventh schedule to the *Transfer of Land Act* 1958 (Vic) reads:

The purchaser or his solicitor shall . . . within 21 days of the day of sale deliver to the vendor or his solicitor in writing all requisitions or objections (if any) on or to the title or concerning any matter appearing in the particulars or conditions . . .

This sentence, embodied by reference into the vast majority of contracts for the sale of real estate in Victoria, is imperative in its language but, in the event of failure to deliver requisitions, the purchaser will not be liable in damages for breach of contract. The sanction is that the purchaser is deemed to have accepted the vendor's title.[11] The word "may" is preferable to "shall" in the sentence quoted.

Words of obligation

As a word of obligation, "must" is more common in everyday usage than "shall" and, in Victoria, "must" is now used in preference to "shall" in statutes and regulations. "Must" can be used to express obligation in private legal documents:

The Mortgagor must produce to the Mortgagee on demand the policy for the insurance of the mortgaged property.

The imperative nature of the sentence is conveyed.

Differing views about whether or not "shall" should be superseded by "must" in private legal documents have recently been expressed in the Australian Law Journal. Professor Eagleson and Ms Asprey[12] have advocated replacing "shall", in its obligatory sense, with "must". They point out that "must" has become the normal auxiliary to express obligation and that "shall" is no longer used in that sense in everyday English but is used to express the future. They consider that legal documents should follow general usage: "In the interests of our clients and ourselves we must stop using 'shall'."

Mr J M Bennett[13] has defended the use of "shall", pointing to its long history, centuries of judicial interpretation and the flexibility that this has brought about. Mr Jim Main[14] writes that he is pleased to have banished "shall" from his office and now uses "must".

The flexibility attributed to "shall" suggests that the document in question is being construed by a court. The fact that it has been referred to a court may be the result of poor drafting. The drafter should ensure, so far as practicable, that the document is clear and comprehensive enough not to require judicial elucidation.

It is fair to say that those who are engaged in business are familiar with the use of "shall" in an imperative sense and that

11. The courts have rescued purchaser from what might occasionally be a drastic penalty by deciding that a condition of that sort cannot be used to force on a purchaser a title with a substantial defect.
12. 63 ALJ 75; and at 726.
13. 63 ALJ 522; 64 ALJ 168.
14. 63 ALJ 860.

most other people are too. "Shall", unlike "must", has a history of use in different senses and this has caused confusion as the illustrations in this chapter show.

Either "shall" or "must" may be used in private legal documents to express obligation. It is for the drafter to ensure that they are used properly "Must" may be more appropriate in documents connected with consumer transactions.

8
Problems of "And" and "Or"

The words "and" and "or" have shades of meaning. Possibilities for ambiguity may arise from the careless use of either of them. The function which each of them is performing may be apparent from the context. Care is required whenever "and" and "or" is used, so that any chance of confusion or ambiguity is eliminated. Where there is any possibility of doubt, the wording should be changed so as to avoid it.

Although it is sometimes said that, in construing a document, a court will read, or substitute, "and" for "or" or "or" for "and", it is more accurate, in most cases, to say that the court is ascertaining the expressed intention of the parties from an examination of the document as a whole. A court may interpret "or" as "and", if it decides, from the context, that the wrong word has been used. This explanation was given by Jessel MR in *Morgan v Thomas*:[1]

> "You will find it said in some cases that 'or' means 'and'; but 'or' never does mean 'and' unless there is a context which shows that it is used for 'and' by mistake . . . It is not that the word has a different meaning from that which it usually bears, but the context shows that the testator has by mistake used one word for another."

Drafters should not leave it to the court to correct their mistakes.

Ambiguity could be avoided by setting out at length the permutations and combinations denoted by an expression containing "and" or "or" but such prolixity would often be unacceptable. For:

1. (1882) 9 QBD 643 at 645.

I give to X all my articles of personal or domestic use or ornament.

the testator could write:

I give to X all my articles of personal use, all my articles of personal ornament, all my articles of domestic use and all my articles of domestic ornament.

"And"

In ordinary usage "and" has a conjunctive effect. For instance, where a testator makes a bequest to "my nephews and nieces", the persons answering the description of my nephew or my niece make up the class of persons to whom the bequest is made.

Nevertheless, the context may require that "and" be construed as having an operation which is not conjunctive. For example, a proviso for re-entry in a sublease exercisable by the sublessor *and* the head lessor enables *either* the sublessor *or* the head lessor to re-enter on breach of covenant.[2] Similarly, it has been decided that a power to apply capital money for "the benefit and advancement" of a life tenant enables the money to be applied as a benefit in circumstances which would not constitute an advancement.[3] Where a power is conferred, as to apply moneys for the benefit and advancement of a life tenant, the expression may be regarded as defining the scope of the power so that any act within that scope is authorised by it.

An instance of the difficulty of ascertaining the meaning of the word "and" occurred in *Associated Artists Ltd v Inland Revenue Commissioners*.[4] The objects of a non-profit-making theatrical association included the following subclause:

"(a) to present classical, artistic, cultural and educational dramatic works".

Upjohn J decided that the subclause must be read disjunctively so that the company could put on a play which was artistic but not educational. The "and" had the effect of aggregating the various classes of works and not making cumulative the characteristics which the work must have. As no charitable concept could be given

---

2. *Doe d Bedford v White* (1827) 4 Bing 276; 130 ER 773.
3. *Re Brittlebank* (1881) 30 WR 99.
4. [1956] 1 WLR 752.

to the word "artistic" in the context, the objects were not exclusively charitable and the association was unable to claim a tax exemption.

"And" joining two or more adjectives

Many cases on the interpretation of "and" linking two or more adjectives illustrate frustration of the intentions of philanthropic testators because the testamentary trusts were so framed that the trustees had the choice of benefiting objects which were not charitable in the legal sense, as well as those which were: the whole trust was void for uncertainty. These decisions have been followed by ameliorating legislation in many jurisdictions.[5] In *Re Best*[6] the trust was upheld: a trust for "charitable and benevolent institutions" was held to mean institutions that were both charitable and benevolent. *Re Eades*[7] shows that it is not strictly correct to say that "and" has a disjunctive sense in the passage that was in issue in this case: "religious charitable and philanthropic objects" to be selected by the trustees. This was the analysis of Sargant J in *Re Eades*:[8]

> **"But is this gift confined by the language of the will to objects that are necessarily 'charitable', in the technical sense of that term? The word 'philanthropic' by itself is undoubtedly too wide, and to render the gift good one must hold that every object of the gift should, in addition to the qualification of being 'philanthropic', have the further qualification of being either 'religious' or 'charitable' or both. Now it is plainly inadmissible to read the words as requiring one only of these two further characteristics, that is as denoting objects which, in addition to being philanthropic, are also either religious or charitable. And the only possible constructions are therefore two, the first being one on which all the objects are to be both religious and charitable and philanthropic; and the second**

5. Vic: *Property Law Act* 1958, s 131.
   NSW: *Conveyancing Act* 1919, s 37D.
   Qld: *Trusts Act* 1973, s 104.
   SA: *Trustee Act* 1936, s 69a.
   WA: *Trustees Act* 1962, s 102.
6. [1904] 2 Ch 354.
7. [1920] 2 Ch 353.
8. Ibid at 356, 357.

being one on which religious objects, and charitable objects and philanthropic objects are within the area of selection—but it is not necessary that any single object should have more than one of these three characteristics.

Such a construction as the second is sometimes referred to as a disjunctive construction, and as involving the change of the word 'and' into 'or'. This is a short and compendious way of expressing the result of the construction, but I doubt whether it indicates accurately the mental conception by which the result is reached. That conception is one, I think, which regards the word 'and' as used conjunctively and by way of addition, for the purpose of enlarging the number of objects within the area of selection; and it does not appear to be a false mental conception, or one really at variance with the ordinary use of language, merely because it involves in the result that the qualifications for selection are alternative or disjunctive.

Further, the greater the number of the qualifications or characteristics enumerated, the more probable, as it seems to me, is a construction which regards them as multiplying the kinds or classes of objects within the area of selection, rather than as multiplying the number of qualifications to be complied with, and so diminishing the objects within the area of selection. In the present case the ordinary careful student of English language and literature would, I think, almost certainly come to the conclusion that the three epithets here are epithets creating conjunctive or cumulative classes of objects, not epithets creating conjunctive or cumulative qualifications for each object."

The judge found that the expression "religious, charitable and philanthropic objects": included objects that were not charitable. The gift in *Re Eades* could have been valid if it had been for "objects that are philanthropic and also either charitable or religious"—although this might not have been what the testator wanted. A limiting phrase that is sometimes useful is "for religious philanthropic and educational institutions if the purpose of the institutions selected are charitable". The judge held that "religious, charitable and philanthropic objects" was a short way of saying "religious objects, charitable objects and philanthropic objects". The interpretation which he did not accept was that the expression referred to objects which had all three qualities of being religious, charitable and philanthropic.

Several adjectives and several nouns

A number of adjectives, the last two joined by "and", followed by a number of nouns, caused doubt in the New Zealand will considered by the Privy Council in *Attorney-General (New Zealand) v Brown*.[9] The testator left a fund in trust for such "charitable benevolent religious and educational institutions societies associations and objects" as his trustees should select. In the judgment[10] it was said that:

> **"It is impossible to use the word 'and' as a link intended to join all the words together and make the gift available only for such institutions or objects as satisfied each one of the conditions represented by each of the separate words. Apart from the fact that such a restriction would all but render the gift inoperative, it is plain from the use of the word 'and' in the phrase 'institutions societies associations and objects' which occurs twice in immediate succession to the words in question, 'and' must be regarded as 'or'."**

On the analysis in *Re Eades*, "and" in the quoted passage is used to extend the class of possible objects and is grammatically correct. If "or" was used the meaning would be the same.

The phrase "articles of domestic use or ornament" would almost certainly be held to have the same meaning as "articles of domestic use and ornament". The former includes in the class all articles which have one at least of the qualities of domestic use or of domestic ornament. The latter aggregates in the class articles of two categories: articles of domestic use and articles of domestic ornament. The mental processes differ but the result is the same. "And" and "or" are correctly used in each case. A different construction could be argued for: articles of domestic use and ornament could be claimed to mean articles that were both useful and ornamental. This construction would very probably be excluded by the context.

Where doubt is foreseen as to the sense in which "and" will be read, the meaning should be made clear.

In a provision enabling a party "his executors administrators and assigns" to waive a breach, "and" would have to be read as "or" to give effect to the words: "or" should have been written instead

9. [1917] AC 393.
10. Ibid at 397.

of "and". But in a covenant intended to bind executors administrators and assigns, as well as the covenantor himself, the covenantor should covenant "for himself his executors administrators and assigns".

Where "and" is used to join adjectives, its conjunctive sense, if this is intended, can be manifested by use of "both . . . and . . .": Objects [which are] both philanthropic and charitable.

Choice between several nouns

Where there are several terms A, B and C such as "religious objects, charitable objects and philanthropic objects" joined conjunctively and it is intended to express a choice between a group containing all of them, groups containing only two of them (A and B but not C, A and C but not B, B and C but not A), and any one of them alone, this can be expressed by saying *any one or more of A and B and C,* or *all or any one or more of A and B and C,* or (as "any" has both a singular and a plural sense) *all or any of A and B and C* or *A and B and C or any of them.* "Every or any of" is a phrase which can be used.

Placing "and" in enumeration

Care must be taken in placing "and" in an enumeration if some of the terms are in a group distinct from the others. In "AB the chairman of directors of the company, CD *and* EF, its other directors, *and* GH, IJ, and KL, members of its staff", there is a correct use of the first "and" to couple CD and EF as "its other directors", and of the second "and" to introduce the group GH and IJ and KL, who alone are described as "members of its staff".

Positive and negative statement

"And" in a positive statement changes to "or" in the negative. "There were cattle and sheep in the pound." "There were no cattle or sheep in the pound."

"Or"

The English language, unlike Latin, does not have separate words for the exclusive "or" (A or B but not both) and the inclusive "or" (A or B or both). The drafter must be particularly careful when using "or" if wanting to avoid ambiguity. "Or" in "either . . . or . . ." is an exclusive "or" but the construction is limited to a choice of two things.

In Garrow's *Law of Wills and Administration*, it is stated:

> " 'Or' is a word of considerable flexibility in its use but the fundamental meaning is always that of an alternative or contrast or a substitution. The precise effect of connecting words, phrases or clauses by 'or' will depend on the context. For the purpose of this chapter its use will be considered under the following heads: (1) as introducing an original gift by way of substitution, (2) as introducing a synonymous or explanatory expression, (3) in enumerating persons, things, or qualifications for some purpose, as for selection or distribution. 'Or' is used also to indicate purely exclusive alternatives, as in the expression 'a fine of two pounds or a week's imprisonment'."

"Or" in substitutional sense

A gift in a will to "A or his children" has been held to be not void for uncertainty, "or" being interpreted in its substitutional sense; if A is alive he takes to the exclusion of his children; if he is not alive, his children take. However, in a devise of real estate such expressions as "or his heirs" or "or his issue" may be treated as the equivalent of "and his heirs" or "and his issue", words of limitation and not of substitution.[11] It is better to say:

To A if he survives me but, if not, to his children.

"Or" in selective sense

An instance of the use of "or" in selective phrases is in a power to appoint to "A, B and C or their children"; on such language it has been held that the donee of the power can select any of A, B and C to the exclusion of any of their children, and any of their children to the exclusion of the parents, or partly from parents and partly from children. To be quite clear you can express the power as being to appoint to

11. *Re Clerke* [1915] 2 Ch 301; *Re Whitehead* [1920] 1 Ch 298; *Re Hayden* [1931] 2 Ch 333.

such one or more exclusively of the others or other of A and B and C and their children as the donee may choose.

It was the use of "or" in selective phrases which gave rise to the decision in *Chichester Diocesan Board v Simpson*,[12] where the phrase used was "for such charitable institution or institutions or other charitable or benevolent object or objects in England" as the executors might select. This was another case of the executors having power to select non-charitable objects resulting in failure of the gift.

"Or" between two words, whether exclusive

"Or" between two words may not be free from ambiguity.

The stock now in the pound are cattle or sheep.

Does this mean (1) that they are either all cattle or all sheep, or does it mean (2) that some are cattle and some are sheep? "Cattle and sheep" would have meaning (2). By using "cattle and/or sheep", the necessity for saying what the stock are is avoided. However objectionable the phrase may be in certain contexts, the meaning of the following interrogatory is clear:

State whether the stock now in the pound are cattle and/or sheep.

If the facts are known, the answer must be:

some are cattle and others are sheep,

or

all are cattle,

or

all are sheep,

or as the case may be.

Here is an instance where "or" might seem to imply one term to the exclusion of others. A trustee is directed to "apply the fund for or towards the maintenance education advancement or benefit of A": does this mean there can be application of the fund for one only of these purposes without application for any others, or does it include application for two or three or all of them? In this context doubt can be avoided by writing:

12. [1944] AC 341.

> **from time to time to apply the fund for or towards the maintenance education advancement or benefit of A.**

Here, every time a payment is made, it may be for a different one of the four purposes. Another expression is:

> **from time to time to apply the fund for or towards the maintenance education advancement and benefit of A or for any [one or more] of those purposes,**

which would leave no doubt that any payment could be made for one, or for any two or three, or for all of the purposes.

However, in the case of a continuing trust, there could be little doubt that "to apply the fund for or towards the maintenance, education, advancement or benefit of A" would authorise expenditure under any of those four headings.

In *Federal Steam Navigation Co v Department of Trade*,[13] the House of Lords had difficulty in determining whether both the owner and the master of a ship, or only one of them, could be guilty of an offence under legislation in these terms:

> **If any oil . . . is discharged from a British ship, the owner or master of the ship shall . . . be guilty of an offence under this section.**

A majority held that "or" was used in a conjunctive sense and that both the owner and the master could be convicted. Lord Wilberforce remarked: "In logic, there is no rule which requires that 'or' should carry an exclusive force. Whether it does so depends on the context."

Comma before last connective in enumeration

Russell recommends that when an enumeration ends with two members separated by "and" or "or" there should be a comma after the last member but one. Current usage, he says, tends to omit a comma in this position, but a comma makes clear that the last two members (when connected by "and") are separate words and not a phrase. For example:

> **"disposition" includes assignment, subletting, and parting with possession.**

13. [1974] 2 All ER 97.

If there is no comma after "subletting", it is not clear whether subletting alone without parting with possession, or parting with possession alone without subletting, is a disposition. Where any ambiguity is possible, the comma should be inserted; otherwise, in conformity with current usage, the comma may be omitted.

"And" and "or" can be confused with each other in dictating or typing or because of careless drafting. In *Re Horrocks*,[14] it was claimed, although found not to have been proved by sufficiently cogent evidence, that a solicitor had dictated "charitable and benevolent object or objects" but the typewritten will read "charitable or benevolent object or objects". Under English law, as it then applied, the trust failed.

"And/or"

The expression "and/or" has been in use in business documents for at least a century and a half. Its meaning was discussed in a case in 1855.[15] It has been criticised by judges. Bennett J[16] stated that it should not be used in an affidavit and threatened to order costs against anyone who did so. In *Bonitto v Fuerst Bros*,[17] Viscount Simon, in discussing the confusion in the pleadings, spoke of "the repeated use of that bastard conjunction 'and/or' which has, I fear, become the commercial court's contribution to basic English".

In *Millen v Grove*,[18] a notice to quit under the *National Security (Landlord and Tenant) Regulations* gave as the ground for terminating the tenancy that the premises were reasonably required by the lessor "for her personal occupation and/or for the occupation of some person who ordinarily resides with and is wholly or partly dependent upon her". Gavan Duffy J said that "the draftsman invited trouble by the common and deplorable affection for the form 'and/or' " but he thought that the notice substantially stated the two grounds provided for in the regulations, namely the premises being required for her personal occupation *and* for the occupation of some person, etc.

14. [1939] p 198.
15. *Cuthbert v Cumming* (1855) 10 Exch 809; 156 ER 668.
16. Practice Note [1940] WN 155.
17. [1944] AC 75 at 82.
18. [1945] VLR 259.

Scrutton LJ considered the ordinary business meaning of "and/or" in *Gurney v Grimer*:[19]

> **There is really a clear understanding of what the words "and/or" mean. To take one of the simplest cases and an obvious case, where there is a charter party by which a ship is to proceed to Rotterdam and/or Antwerp at charterer's option it means one of three things: the charterer may either send the vessel to Rotterdam alone or he may send her to Antwerp alone, or he may send her to Rotterdam and Antwerp.**

"And/or" has required judicial elucidation in a number of cases, suggesting that there is a risk of confusion if the expression is used.

In *Re Griffiths*,[20] Mann J held that a trust to distribute a fund "amongst other persons than my said near relatives and/or charitable institutions or organisations" meant a trust to distribute in any of the following ways: (1) partly among "other persons than my said near relatives" and partly among "charitable institutions or organisations", or (2) wholly among "other persons than my said near relatives", or (3) wholly among "charitable institutions or organisations". This interpretation accords with that of Scrutton LJ quoted above.

"And/or" occurred in the will considered in *Re Lewis*,[21] where Farwell J had to decide the effect of a gift to "Margaret Ann and/or John Richards". He said:

> **"The expression 'and/or' is unfortunate. I do not think I have met it before in a will, and I hope I shall never meet it again. I have, however, to put a meaning on it, if possible. . . . I think that the testator meant that Margaret Ann and John Richards should take the residue as joint tenants, but that, if Margaret Ann did not survive the testator, the gift to John Richards was to take effect in substitution for the joint gift. In the events which have happened, the residue goes to them as joint tenants, and I make a declaration accordingly."**

Margaret Ann and John Richards had both survived the testator. The judgment does not state what would have been the effect of "Margaret Ann and/or John Richards" if John Richards had not survived and Margaret Ann had.

---

19. (1932) 38 Comm Cas 7 at 13.
20. [1926] VLR 212 at 219.
21. [1942] Ch 424.

Williams J commented unfavourably on the use of "and/or" in *Fadden v Deputy Federal Commission of Taxation*:[22]

"In the case of the Bank of New South Wales the accounts were opened in the name of the deceased and/or a daughter, an elliptical and embarrassing expression which endangers accuracy for the sake of brevity."

He considered that it meant: "to be at the disposal of either during the joint lives and upon the death of either at the disposal of the survivor".

Commercial cases illustrate difficulties that can arise from using "and/or".

In *Furness v Tennant*,[23] the obligation to load "a full and complete cargo of sugar in hogsheads and (or) bags, or other lawful merchandise" was held to be discharged by loading a cargo of sugar either in hogsheads or in bags or partly in hogsheads and partly in bags.

Cuthbert v Cumming[24] was a decision on a contract "to load a full and complete cargo of sugar, molasses, and/or other lawful produce". Alderson B held that the parties were either (1) to load a full and complete cargo of sugar and molasses and other lawful produce or, (2) a full and complete cargo of sugar and molasses, or (3) a full and complete cargo of other lawful produce. By implication a full and complete cargo of sugar alone or molasses alone would not have satisfied the contractual obligation but the question did not need to be decided.

However, in *Stanton v Richardson*,[25] on a charterparty by which a ship was to load a cargo of "sugar in bags, hemp in compressed bales, and/or measurement goods", it was held that a cargo made up only of sugar in bags was within the contract.

"And/or" disturbs run of sentence

And/or disturbs the reader.

"To use as one a word that links conjunctively and a word that links disjunctively does not make for clearness. 'And/or' may

22. (1943) 68 CLR 76 at 82.
23. (1892) 66 LT 635.
24. (1855) 10 Exch 809; 156 ER 668.
25. (1875) 45 LJQB 78.

be a much less simple formula to fit into the meaning of a sentence than such a phrase as 'with or without'. To pass and repass 'with horses and/or cattle and/or pigs' are words not quite so easily understood as to pass and repass 'with horses cattle and pigs or any of them'. So it is that a sentence that otherwise runs smoothly may suddenly hold up its reader even by an 'and/or', and if there are several he may make a long pause before he can take in all the possible meanings.''[26]

The point taken in this comment seems well founded. It is the drafter's duty to be clear; anything that takes the reader's attention from the straightforward run of the sentence hinders a ready understanding of it.

Careless use of "and/or"

"And/or" can be used carelessly in sentences in which it adds nothing to the meaning or in which its use is absurd.

Any increase in costs and/or taxation will reduce the net return.

The assured are not to be prejudiced by the presence of the negligence clause and/or the patent defect clause in the bill of lading.

"Or" would be sufficient in each case.

The use of "and/or" is absurd in:

If the ship is totally destroyed by fire in the Pacific Ocean and/or the Mediterranean.

Information disclosed by the member and/or the legal personal repesentative of the member.

More than one "and/or"

Commercial documents sometimes contain more than one "and/or" in a series of terms. Thus a marine policy described the risk as goods to be shipped:

at and from port or ports, place and/or places in the United Kingdom and/or Continent of Europe and/or United States of America and/or Canada to port or ports place and/or places in Australia and/or Tasmania.

26. (1933) 7 ALJ 76.

Ascertaining the meaning of a sentence containing multiple and/or's can be difficult and, in any case, time consuming. There may be doubt about the correct construction.

Conclusion

"And/or" is best discarded. It does not significantly improve brevity. It makes a passage less easy to follow and it can, especially where there is more than one, cause doubt and confusion. It is not correct English. The courts have not regarded the expression favourably. This is another reason for avoiding it.

9
Various Words and Constructions

Provisos

Once provisos were used frequently in legal composition, but their use is declining. It is better not to use them at all.

They have been used to vary or modify a general rule in its application to particular circumstances. The proviso is introduced by the formula "provided that" or by similar expressions such as "provided always that" or "provided nevertheless that".

> **Notice of exercise of the option shall be delivered to the grantor of the option at her residential address stated above provided that if the grantor has died the notice shall be delivered to her solicitors.**

"Proviso" is to be distinguished from "provision" which means anything contained in the operative part of a document.

"Provided", as a past participle, has an adjectival application corresponding to "provision" rather than to "proviso" and meaning "set out" or "agreed".

> **The vendor may give notice to the purchaser in the manner provided in clause 2.**

Coode attacked the proviso describing it as "That bane of all correct composition" and modern writers on drafting have recommended its avoidance.[1] Robinson points out that the proviso has evolved from the enacting words of earlier English statutes: Provisum est: it is provided. These words were used to introduce an independent section of a statute. The insertion in a sentence of a passage commencing: "provided that . . ." is ungrammatical.

1. Robinson (1980), pp 43 et seq. Dick (1972), pp 90 et seq.

Coode says of the proviso:[2]

> "At present the abuse of the formula is universal. Formerly they were used in an intelligible manner; where a general enactment had preceded, but a special case occurred for which a distinct and special enactment was to be made, different from the general enactment, this latter enactment was made by way of proviso . . .
>
> Nothing has inflicted more trouble on the judges than the attempt to give a construction to provisos. The courts have generally assumed, in accordance with the old practice just described, that a proviso was a mode of enactment by which the general operation of a statute was excluded in favour of some case. There are, therefore, in their decisions, various distinctions propounded between mere exemptions, or exceptions, or salvos and proper provisos. But it is admitted by all writers to be impossible to make any general application of the doctrines laid down by the courts to the multitude of cases in which the formula of a proviso has been adopted.

Coode's advice has already been referred to, that an exception should be expressed as such and in the part of the sentence to which it relates, rather than by means of a proviso at the end of the sentence.[3] If certain persons are to be excluded from the operation of a provision, this should be expressed as an exception in the description of those persons. If certain circumstances are to be excluded from those in which the provision is to operate, the "case", this should be expressed as an exception to those circumstances, as an exception to the case.

Another use of the proviso which is criticised is its use as a means of introducing consecutive provisions. The introduction of each provision with some such formula as "provided that" or "provided that and it is hereby agreed", may represent an endeavour by the drafter to ensure that those provisions are governed by words imposing an obligation but in most documents words imposing an obligation on the parties will appear at the beginning of the operative part and, even if they were required, some words other than "provided that" would be more appropriate: "it is agreed"; "the parties agree". Where "provided

2. Coode (1843), p xxv.
3. See above, p 27.

that" is used in this manner, it is surplus and can be omitted altogether. Sometimes it can be replaced by "and".

On the use of the proviso, Coode also says:

"Whenever matter is seen by the writer to be incapable of being generally expressed in connexion with the rest of any clause, he thrusts it in with a proviso. Whenever he perceives a disparity, an anomaly, an inconsistency or a contradiction, he introduces it with a 'provided always'."

Traditional use of provisos

Some documents are traditionally in a form that involves the use of the proviso. Doubtless they could be framed, and might be better framed, without one. Examples are mortgages of general law or old system land, and leases.

The traditional mortgage contains a conveyance of the mortgaged property to the lender subject to a proviso for redemption introduced by "provided that" or a similar expression and setting out the condition that, upon payment of the mortgage debt, interest and costs, the lender will reconvey the mortgaged property to the borrower.

In a lease, the formal grant of the term of years, covenants by the parties and agreements between them, will usually be followed by a clause in the form of a proviso, introduced by such words as "Provided always and it is agreed" under which the landlord may terminate the lease on notice in the event of the tenant's default or, perhaps, without notice in certain eventualities.

These uses of the proviso are traditional and do not make the document difficult to understand, although a different grammatical construction is preferable and is available. In addition to these traditional uses of the proviso, it was once common to introduce with the proviso formula, "provided that" or its equivalent, other material such as the manner of service of notices, the removal of fixtures at the end of the term or responsibility for water damage, to each of which Coode's objections apply that these are not matters of limitation or qualification, but are matters of agreement that should appear as such in a clause containing agreements only and should be introduced, if words imposing an obligation are needed, by some such formula as "the parties agree".

This testamentary disposition, containing a proviso, was construed by the court in *Re Potter* deceased:[4]

I GIVE DEVISE and BEQUEATH my house property situated at .... to my daughter .... for her own use and benefit absolutely PROVIDED that my said son .... may reside in the said house so long as he so desires.

Menhennit J held that the daughter took an estate in fee simple to the house property subject to a trust in favour of the son under which he had the right to reside personally in the house for so long as he wished but not to the exclusion of the daughter. It might have saved recourse to the Supreme Court if, instead of using a proviso, the drafter had been able to define the interests which the daughter and the son were intended to take.

Provisos open to objection

The use of the proviso is traditional, but not necessary, in general law mortgages: the proviso for redemption; and in leases: the proviso for re-entry. It is interesting that the power to re-enter implied (unless excluded) in a lease registered under s 67(1)(d) of the Victorian *Transfer of Land Act* 1958 is not cast in the form of a proviso.

Because of the difficulties of construction which provisos can give rise to, their ungrammatical nature and their flavour of legalese, it is best to avoid using them.

"Subject to"

"Subject to" is a phrase whereby one provision, the master provision, can be expressed to prevail over another, the subject provision. If clause 7 commences with the words "Subject to clause 6", any inconsistency between the clauses will be resolved in favour of the master clause, clause 6. Similarly, if subclause (1) begins with "Subject to subclause (4)", then, in so far as subclause (1) clashes with subclause (4), subclause (4) will prevail.

Megarry J, in *C & J Clark Ltd v IRC*[5] said:

"In my judgment, the phrase 'Subject to' is a simple provision which merely subjects the provisions of the subject subsections

4. [1970] VR 352.
5. [1973] 1 WLR 905 at 911.

to the provisions of the master subsections. Where there is no clash, the phrase does nothing; if there is a collision, the phrase shows what is to prevail. The phrase provides no warranty of universal collision."

"Subject to" may be used by the drafter out of an abundance of caution: the two provisions concerned need not be inconsistent.

"Subject to" can be used in wills, settlements and other instruments creating interests in succession.

An article in the *Australian Law Journal*,[6] points out that "subject to", in wills, has two principal uses. The first is when a gift has been made of part of a fund and it is desired to dispose of what remains; the second is when it is intended that any prior gift that lapses shall pass with the gift of the balance; in either case, "subject to" can be used to introduce the gift of the balance. Both uses of "subject to" are illustrated by the example given in the article:

> **"(a) As to one third of my residuary estate upon trust for A if he is alive at my death;**
>
> **(b) As to another one third upon trust for B if he is then alive;**
>
> **(c) Subject to the foregoing trusts (*or*, 'Subject to paragraphs (a) and (b)') to hold my residuary estate upon trust for C."**

The article continues:

> "The effect of the last paragraph is to give C the remaining one third if the trusts in paragraphs (a) and (b) take effect (this is what we called the first use of 'subject to'); and also—this is its second use—if the trusts in one or both of paragraphs (a) and (b) fail, to give him also the part or parts to which those trusts relate. It is much shorter and safer to use this form of words than to attempt to set out the circumstances in which C will take either one third or two thirds or the whole of the fund."

An example of a failure to set out every circumstance in which a gift is intended to take effect appears to be provided by the will which gave rise to the decision in *Re Bailey*.[7] The testatrix gave

6. (1938) 12 ALJ 51.
7. [1951] Ch 407.

her residuary estate on trust for her daughter for life, and after the daughter's death for her sister-in-law if she should survive the daughter, but, if she should predecease the daughter, for her nephew. First the daughter, and then the sister-in-law, died during the lifetime of the testatrix, and the nephew, as the only beneficiary to survive the testatrix, claimed her residuary estate.

The nephew argued that the testatrix must have intended him to have the residuary estate as it could not pass to the sister-in-law since she had predeceased the testatrix. However, a gift on a contingency does not take effect unless the exact contingency occurs. The court held that, because the contingency on which the nephew was to take, that the sister-in-law should predecease the daughter, had not occurred, the gift to the nephew failed.

The testatrix would most probably have wished her residuary estate to pass to her nephew, but she and her advisers overlooked the possibility that the sister-in-law might survive the daughter but predecease the testatrix. This is an excellent example of a case in which the ultimate gift to the nephew might best have been made "subject to" the dispositions in favour of the daughter and sister-in-law, so that there would be no need to try to express every possible contingency.

"Subject as aforesaid", a legalistic term, has a similar use. In *Macpherson v Maund*,[8] Latham CJ said that the words "subject as aforesaid", used in a will after dispositions have been made, and introducing another disposition, mean "subject to the operation of preceding dispositions, so far as they do operate". Similar reasoning was applied in *Re Edwards' Will Trusts*.[9] A less legalistic and less vague substitute is "Subject to the preceding provisions of this instrument" (or, "of this clause" or "of this paragraph"), or "Subject to clause 6(f)", and is to be preferred.

"Supplemental"

Where an instrument varies or adds to an earlier instrument, or is subordinate to it in some other way, repetition of the previous instrument by recital in the later one can be avoided in most jurisdictions by expressing the later instrument to be *supplemental*

8. (1937) 58 CLR 341.
9. [1948] Ch 440.

to the previous one. The Victorian *Property Law Act* 1958, s 58,[10] provides that:

> "Any instrument (whether executed before or after the commencement of this Act) expressed to be supplemental to a previous instrument, shall, as far as may be, be read and have effect as if the supplemental instrument contained a full recital of the previous instrument."

For the purpose of the section, "instrument" is defined as including a deed or a will. The ordinary meaning of the term, formal legal document, would also apply.

Use of active voice

Verbs expressing the legal action should preferably be in the active voice. It is then clear on whom is imposed the duty of performing the legal action.

A *passive or impersonal form* may leave the legal consequences in doubt. It is one thing to say "A shall give notice", and another that "notice shall be given": the latter may leave in doubt who is to give the notice. A stipulation in a lease that "nothing shall be done to the detriment annoyance or inconvenience of the landlord" may not have the same effect as a covenant by the tenant that "I will not do or suffer to be done anything to the detriment annoyance or inconvenience of the landlord". If there is a clause enabling the landlord to determine the tenancy upon breach of a covenant by the tenant, and the facts are that annoyance has been caused to the landlord not by the tenant's own act but by something that the tenant has permitted to be done or neglected to prevent, the landlord, if the first form of expression is used, may fail to establish that there has been a breach of covenant.

"Any"

"Any" has been described as a word that "excludes limitation or qualification"; its sense is "as wide as possible". Williams J in *Victorian Chamber of Manufactures v Commonwealth*[11] said:

> any is a word which ordinarily excludes limitation or qualification and which should be given as wide a construction

10. The *New South Wales Conveyancing Act*, s 36D is to the same effect.
11. (1943) 67 CLR 335 at 346.

as possible. "Any goods" therefore includes "all goods" except where the wide construction is limited by the subject matter and context of a particular statute.

"Any" has both a singular and a plural sense; also it may mean "all". "Any of A, B and C", unless controlled by its context, will mean A alone or B alone or C alone, or any two of them, or all three of them.

"Either" is usually more suitable than "any" where only two persons are involved:

Either A or B may sign cheques on behalf of the partnership.

"Any" also has a recurring sense, making the sentence applicable from time to time whenever a situation recurs:

Any director may convene a meeting of the board.

Here "any" has a singular sense but the sentence takes effect whenever a director wants to call a board meeting.

A will provides: "the money to my credit at the time of my death in any bank". This expression would cover money to the credit of the testator in a number of banks. "Any" has a plural sense in this context. It would not be necessary to invoke s 61 of the *Property Law Act* 1958[12] under which the singular would include the plural, unless the context otherwise required, and "any bank" would be equivalent to "any bank or banks".

There is a tendency to overdo the use of "any" in drafting. The indefinite article may carry the same meaning and will then be equally appropriate, perhaps more so, as it sounds more natural. "Any" can be reserved for provisions whose universitality it is desirable to emphasise.

Negatives

In *Psychological Aspects of Negation*,[13] it is asserted that there is "now substantial evidence . . . to show that in making inferences or drawing conclusions people grasp and use 'negative information' much less efficiently than positive information." It

---

12. See above, p 52.
13. Published by Communications Research Centre at University College, London. See also 59 LS Gaz at 634.

describes the mental gymnastics of a recipient of negative information who, in the process of comprehending it, will translate it into positive form, resulting in delay and perhaps a wrong conclusion.

Where a statement can be expressed with equal felicity in the positive or the negative, the positive should be preferred.

Difficulty in comprehension is increased where there is more than one negative in the sentence.

The negative will be needed in many cases where there is no alternative: Cars may not enter X street between 7 am and 9 am.

A trust's investments are to be valued at intervals of not more than two years unless the trustee and the beneficiaries agree to waive this requirement. This passage is hard to follow and may not give full effect to the intentions of the settlor who probably wished any waiver to apply only to a particular year and not to be general:

The investments need not be valued at intervals of not more than two years if the trustee and the beneficiaries so agree.

This is an alternative which is easier to understand:

The trustee and the beneficiaries may, in any year, agree to waive the requirement that the investments be valued in that year.

"Less than" and "more than"

When using "less than" and "more than" in a list of periods, quantities or charges it is possible to leave a hiatus. If compensation payable in respect of late completion of work varies with the period of delay, this list is incorrect:

Less than 7 days	**$100**
More than 7 days but less than 14 days	**$200**
More than 14 days but less than 21 days	**$300**

It should read:

Not exceeding 7 days	**$100**
Exceeding 7 days but not exceeding 14 days	**$200**
Exceeding 14 days but not exceeding 21 days	**$300**

Similar problems can arise with dates. See below, p 117.

"Either"

If a will contains this passage:

If either my son or my daughter dies in my lifetime leaving a child or children alive at my death the child or children shall take the share which the parent would have taken

and both the son and the daughter die leaving children, does the clause take effect in favour of the children of each of them? In other words does "either" mean here "one but not both", or does it mean "one or both"? The latter would be intended; and so it would be better to use "one or both".

There was a problem of this sort in *Re Pickworth*:[14]

"if either of my said sisters shall be then dead . . . upon trust for the survivor of my said sisters absolutely."

Both sisters were then dead. The court was able to solve the problem by looking at other passages of the will. Lindley MR said:[15]

" 'either' may mean 'both', as when you say 'on either side of the road there is a public-house'—that means on each side. Especially in a negative sentence it is pretty plain that 'either' means or includes both in the sense of each; but I do not think that the expression 'if either of my said sisters shall be then dead' can be taken as expressing in common English the contingency of both being dead."

Rigby LJ dissenting, said, at 650, that the prima facie meaning of "either" was "one or other", not "one only".

This case shows the importance of dealing with contingencies which can be reasonably foreseen and of expressing intention clearly.

Issue

The meaning of the word "issue" is "descendants of any degree". The word is not synonymous with children. Its use instead of "children" may frustrate a settlor's or testator's intentions and may even invalidate a gift. It should be avoided unless it is required

14. [1899] 1 Ch 642.
15. Ibid at 648.

by the client's instructions and then its meaning and effect should be explained.

The question whether a disposition infringed the rule against remoteness of vesting (now modified by legislation in most Australian jurisdictions) was considered by the High Court in *Buick v Equity Trustees Co.*[16]

The testator, after directing that on the death of his wife the income of his estate was to be paid to his children, then went on:

> **"and on the death of any of my children the portion of my real and personal estate to which such deceased child was entitled shall be divided between the *issue* of such child *per stirpes* on each of such *issue* attaining the age of twenty-one years provided that if any child of mine shall die in my lifetime leaving *issue* who shall survive me and who being male shall attain the age of twenty one years or being female shall attain that age or marry under that age such *issue* shall take and if more than one equally between them the share which their his or her parent would have taken of and in my residuary estate if such parent had lived to attain a vested interest".**

Dixon CJ and Kitto J held that "issue" as used in the will meant all lineal descendants and not simply children, and that accordingly the remainder to the "issue" was bad for remoteness. Fullagar J considered that the word "issue" meant "children".

One cannot help wondering whether the word "issue" was ever used by the testator in giving his instructions, or whether it was the drafter who put the word into the testator's mouth, thus stultifying his intention and, in any case, not drawing the will in accordance with his instructions.

If a gift to children is intended, the word "children" should be used. If it is intended to refer to descendants of any degree, it may be clearer to use "children and remoter issue" rather than the word "issue" by itself. Use of the word alone can raise doubt as to the correct interpretation of a document, which can only be resolved by a court.[17]

16. (1957) 97 CLR 599.
17. *Re Wardle* (1979) 23 SASR 214.

"Survive" and *"Survivors"*

Phrases containing these words frequently give rise to questions of construction.[18] In *Re Gregson's Trusts*[19] Sir W P Wood VC said:

> "Certainly this word 'survivor' is one that ought to be avoided by any person who is not a consummate master of the art of conveyancing, for I suppose no word has occasioned more difficulty."

Dixon J said:

> "No-one doubts that the natural meaning of the word 'survive' is to remain alive after the termination of some other continuing thing or after the occurrence of some other event. In short, it means to outlive."[20]

"Survive" was literally interpreted in the recent case of *In the matter of the Will and Estate of Arndt*.[21] There the testatrix directed that a portion of her residuary estate should, after the death of her son, be held in trust for such of the son's children "as shall survive me and attain the age of eighteen (18) years as tenants in common in equal shares". A child of the son born after the death of the testatrix was held not to be entitled to share in the residuary estate.

However, the courts, from an examination of the will as a whole and of the circumstances when it was made, have sometimes been able to find that the testator intended to use the word in a more liberal sense.

In *Re Clark's Estate*,[22] a disposition to

> **"M for life and after her death to all and every the children of the said M who shall survive me"**

was held to include children of M who were born *after* the death of the testator.

The use of the word "survive" in this example could have been avoided and the testator's intention made quite clear, if one of the following phrases had been used:

18. *Brennan v Permanent Trustee Co* (1945) 73 CLR 404. *Wilson v Harris* (1964) 65 SR (NSW) 329.
19. (1864) 33 LJ Ch 532.
20. *Brennan v Permanent Trustee Co* (1945) 73 CLR 404 at 414.
21. [1990] WAR 5; see also 64 ALJ 515.
22. (1864) 3 De GJ & S 111; 46 ER 579.

(if the intention was to include only those born during the testator's lifetime, and alive at his death) "to M for life and after her death to all the children of M who are alive at my death"

or

(if the intention was to include children born after the testator's death) "to M for life and after her death to all the children of M who are alive at or born after my death" or "all the children of M who are alive at her death".

Where there is a gift to "survivors" of a designated person, the word, in its natural meaning, denotes the persons alive at the date at which a gift to the survivors takes effect. There could be no doubt of the meaning of the word in the example

to A and B in equal shares or the survivor of them.

But suppose that the gift is

to X for life, remainder to A and B in equal shares or the survivor of them.

A and B being alive at the testator's death, while A dies during the life of X. Is this a case of the natural meaning, or may there be some indication in the will that the interests of both A and B become vested on their surviving the testator, so that on the death of X the estate of A shares equally with B? Doubt could be avoided by saying

to X for life, remainder to A and B if both are alive at my death (or, at the death of X) or if only one then to that one only.

Joint tenants and tenants in common

A joint tenancy should never be created by inadvertence.

To A for life remainder to such of her children as attain the age of 18 years.

If three children of A attain the age of 18 they will take the remainder as joint tenants since there are no words of severance showing that they are to take separate and distinct shares. Unless the joint tenancy is broken, one child will eventually own the whole of the remainder. This is unlikely to have been intended.

The children would have taken as tenants in common if words of severance had been added to the above disposition, such as "in equal shares", or "equally" or, of course, "as tenants in common in equal shares".

The common law rule that, in the absence of words of severance, the grantees take as joint tenants has been altered by statute[23] in New South Wales, Queensland and the Australian Capital Territory so that, in those jurisdictions, if there are no words of severance, the members of the class will take as tenants in common.

When more than one person is to take an interest, the drafter should ascertain whether they are to take as joint tenants or tenants in common and draw the document accordingly.

"Subject to contract"—preliminary documents

It is common for an informal or preliminary agreement or arrangement to be expressed to be "subject to contract", or "subject to formal contract". It is well settled that the use of such phrases raises a very strong presumption that the parties do not intend to bind themselves legally and consequently in law there is no contract. The matter is still in negotiation.[24] No legal rights or obligations are created.

Documents, apparently recording contracts, but, at the same time, contemplating the execution by the parties of a subsequent formal contract, fall into three categories as was stated by the High Court in *Masters v Cameron*:[25]

First, those in which the parties intend to be bound immediately by the terms to which they have agreed, but at the same time propose to have those terms restated in a form which will be fuller and more precise, but not different in effect. In this case there is a contract binding the parties to perform the agreed terms, whether the formal document intended to be the final repository of their agreement comes into existence or not.

Secondly, those in which the parties have finally agreed upon all the terms and intend no departure from or addition to them, but

---

23. NSW: *Conveyancing Act* 1919, s 26.
    Qld: *Property Law Act* 1974, s 35.
    ACT: *Law of Property (Miscellaneous Provisions) Act* 1958, s 3.
24. *Chillingworth v Esche* [1924] 1 Ch 97.
25. (1954) 91 CLR 353; especially at 360, 361.

yet have made performance of one or more of the terms conditional upon the execution of a formal contract. Here there is a contract which binds the parties to join in bringing the formal contract into existence and then to carry it into execution.

Thirdly, those in which the parties do not intend to make a concluded contract at all unless and until they execute a formal contract. Here there is no enforceable contract. What has been agreed on must be regarded merely as the intended basis for a future contract and not as constituting a legally binding contract.

If the expression "subject to contract" is used, the document is presumed to fall into the third category.[26]

Where the document contemplates the execution of a further agreement, the drafter should state whether or not, or to what extent, the original document is intended to be legally binding.[27]

Discussions between parties to a proposed commercial transaction sometimes give rise to "heads of agreement" recording, often in fairly general terms, the points on which they have agreed. Heads of agreement contemplate the subsequent execution of a more comprehensive formal agreement and whether they themselves amount to a contract in law will depend on the circumstances. They will almost invariably leave some matters unresolved and, in general, it is desirable that the formal agreement be settled, drawn up and executed, as soon as possible. The parties should not be in doubt as to whether the heads of agreement are intended to constitute a legally binding contract. The heads of agreement should state expressly whether or not they are intended to bind the parties legally or whether certain of their provisions (such as a promise to be responsible for the other party's expenses) are intended to be legally binding and others not.

---

26. *Tiverton Estates Ltd v Wearwell Ltd* [1974] 1 All ER 209 at 216-218.
27. See *Von Hatzfeldt-Wildenberg v Alexander* [1912] 1 Ch 284.

10
Drafting Aids

Punctuation

In the English language, which is little inflected, the meaning of
a sentence is derived from the order and grouping of words. The
groupings of words and the pattern of the sentence can be made
evident to the reader by the use of punctuation. Nevertheless,
commas and other marks of punctuation, even full stops, fared
badly at the hands of the older writers and judges. Davidson in
1860[1] wrote:

"The writing of a legal instrument is without punctuation;
such stops and marks of parenthesis must be supplied by the
reader as will give effect to the whole. Marks of parenthesis
are, indeed, usually inserted, but it seems that they are to be
regarded, in the construction of the deed, only when they are
consonant with the sense, and required by the context. The
Precedents in this collection are pointed by the printers,
according to the usual practice; but no attention is to be paid
to the punctuation."

And *Norton on Deeds*[2] has its reference to *Sanford v Raikes*[3] in
which the Master of the Rolls said:

"It is from the words, and from the context, not from the
punctuation, that the sense must be collected."

But there are later authorities to the contrary. The speeches in the
House of Lords in *Houston v Burns*[4] show that the court will look
at the punctuation in a will for the purpose of helping in its
construction—although it may be that the punctuation will be

1. Davidson (1885), Vol I, p 21.
2. Norton (1928), p 100.
3. (1816) 1 Mer 646; 35 ER 808.
4. [1918] AC 337 at 342, 344 and 348.

disregarded if it is contrary to what the court thinks to be the plain meaning of the document. Lord Shaw[5] said: "Punctuation is a rational part of English composition, and is sometimes quite significantly employed. I see no reason for depriving legal documents of such significance as attaches to punctuation in other writings."

> "A comma is one means of expressing intention in a writing, and a court is entitled to have regard to it, though of course not to be controlled by it if the context nevertheless requires otherwise"

said Isaacs J in *Committee of Direction of Fruit Marketing v Collins.*[6]

Perhaps the best statement of the effect of punctuation marks is contained in the following quotation from Burrows, *Words and Phrases Judicially Defined*:

> "The principle applied appears to be that the courts will use punctuation marks appearing in the document and, whenever necessary, supply them, but such marks are only used to assist in understanding the words. If they are without sense or conflict with the plain meaning of the words in the document, the courts will not allow them to cause a meaning to be placed upon such words which they otherwise would not have."

The words used should carry the required meaning, even if they are unpunctuated.

Use of punctuation is desirable

If punctuation marks are used carefully and systematically throughout a private document, in such a way as to show that the parties inserted them as one means of expressing their intention, it seems that a court would not disregard them in any case where they made clear which of two meanings is to be taken, where the choice would otherwise be doubtful. However, if without the punctuation the meaning is clear, the punctuation would not be allowed to disturb it.

Although lawyers made themselves proficient in a style of drafting that states a definite meaning without punctuation, there

5. Ibid at 348.
6. (1925) 36 CLR 410 at 421.

is no question that, in a long sentence, commas, colons, semi-colons and brackets will make the meaning easier to grasp. One way of reducing the use of stops is to adopt a style of drafting arranged in paragraphs and subparagraphs. There can be little doubt that a court, in interpreting a document which showed a systematic use of paragraphs and subparagraphs, numbered and with appropriate margins, would take account of these aids to understanding.

If several names (each made up of given names and surnames) follow one another without other words between them, there should be a comma after each surname, for without commas there may be doubt between given name and surname and so uncertainty as to what the names are:

William Douglas Barry Martin Ross Patrick and John Anderson.

Punctuation is an aid to understanding. It should be used in drafting. The same system of punctuation should be applied consistently throughout the document.

Brackets

Brackets can be used to separate some subordinate statement from the theme of the sentence and also to enclose explanatory or illustrative material or comment. The closing bracket helps the reader to pick up the sentence again. For example:

Upon default by the Borrower, the Lender may without notice (and whether or not a demand for payment has been made in the case of a default consisting of failure to pay money when due) take possession of the mortgaged property.

In this example, the passage in brackets is quite long and the reader tends to lose the run of the sentence but the closing bracket refers the reader back to "may without notice".

Brackets may also be used to interpolate an additional statement:

No alteration shall be made that will in the opinion of the Association (whose decision shall be final) substantially prejudice the rights or interests of any person in respect of any payment already made.

This example is taken from the *Pharmacy Act* 1974 (Vic), s 21(3):

Each pharmacy practice carried on at separate premises (notwithstanding that the pharmacy practice may be carried on under the same business name as another pharmacy practice) shall be a separate pharmacy practice.

Commas can often be used in place of brackets. In the above passage it may have been more correct grammatically to do so. However, the primary object is to express the intended meaning clearly and, in achieving this object, brackets can be useful.

Precautions where punctuation and brackets are used

Where punctuation is used, commas and other punctuation marks should be checked as carefully as the words. Brackets (or parentheses as curved brackets are technically called) should be checked to ensure that where there is a commencing bracket there is also a closing one and that they are in the right place.

This stipulation will ensure that punctuation is taken into account when construing a document:

All marks of punctuation and brackets are to be deemed part of this document and are to be given effect in interpreting it.

The use of such a stipulation is uncommon and it seems that drafters have not found it helpful. If it is used, punctuating the document and checking the punctuation should be carried out meticulously.

Schedules

The use of schedules may improve the design and flow of a document. Lists and other complex or lengthy material may be placed in a schedule, thereby making the document more manageable. A further advantage is that reference to the scheduled material is easier. It may consist, for instance, of a detailed specification of equipment to be supplied by a party. The specification is a unit and is more easily referred to in the schedule than in the body of the document. Again, the material may not be available until a late stage in the negotiations and the parties can draw and settle the document and the schedule can be added at the last minute if necessary.

In an agreement for the acquisition of the share capital of a company, the vendor may be required to enter into covenants which protect the purchaser against the non-disclosure of material information and against liabilities arising after the acquisition out of events that occurred before it. The covenants may cover many pages but are really a protective device. By placing the covenants in a schedule to the agreement, supported by a short clause in the operative part, the agreement will not be unbalanced by the inclusion of many pages of static text.

A deed of family arrangement under which the dispositions of a will were to be varied, would once contain lengthy recitals, including recital of relevant provisions of the will. Recitals can be reduced in length by putting a copy of the will and other relevant material, such as a statement of the deceased's assets and liabilities, in a schedule to the deed. Photocopying makes this simple to do.

The following example is a form of Conveyance in "Conveyancer's Diary" in the *Solicitors' Journal*.[7] It is well drawn but contains one or two terms which would be regarded as old-fashioned to-day. It demonstrates the convenience that results from the use of schedules.

"THIS CONVEYANCE is made the 29th December 1945 between Henry Smith of Bog Cottage, Nomansland, Herts (hereinafter called the vendor) and Robert Curtis of Dale Farm, Aylesbury, Bucks (hereinafter called the purchaser).

WHEREAS

1. The vendor is estate owner in fee simple in possession of the property described in the First Schedule hereto subject to and with the benefit of the lease mentioned in the Second Schedule hereto and with the benefit of the easements mentioned in the Third Schedule hereto, but otherwise free from encumbrances.

2. The vendor has agreed to sell the said premises to the purchaser for £1,000 subject to the purchaser entering into the restrictive covenants hereafter mentioned.

THIS DEED WITNESSES:—

1. In consideration of £1,000 (receipt of which from the purchaser the vendor acknowledges) and of the purchaser's covenant in Clause 2 hereof, the vendor as beneficial owner

---

7. (1945) SJ at 574.

conveys to the purchaser in fee simple the property described in the First Schedule hereto subject to the lease mentioned in the Second Schedule hereto and with the benefit of the easements described in the Third Schedule hereto.

2. The purchaser with intent to bind the land hereby conveyed and every part thereof covenants with the vendor for the benefit of the vendor's land known as Bog Cottage shown on the plan drawn hereon and thereon coloured blue and every part thereof that the purchaser and his successors in title will observe the stipulations set out in the Fourth Schedule hereto.

IN WITNESS etc.

THE FIRST SCHEDULE

All that house and garden at Nomansland Herts known as Clay Cottage which is shown in the plan drawn on this deed and there coloured red.

THE SECOND SCHEDULE

A lease dated 6th February 1942 for five years from 1st January 1942 made between the vendor (1) and Hugh Hopkins (2) at a rent of £52 per year.

THE THIRD SCHEDULE

1. A right in fee simple for the owners or occupiers of Clay Cottage at all reasonable times to enter on foot the garden of the adjacent property known as Manor Farm and to draw water from the well marked W on the said plan.

2. A right in fee simple for the said persons to discharge sewage into the cesspit at the said Manor Farm which is marked C on such plan.

THE FOURTH SCHEDULE

Without leave of the occupier of Bog Cottage—

1. No business shall be carried on at Clay Cottage.

2. No musical instrument may be played nor may any wireless receiving set be operated except with headphones after 10 pm at Clay Cottage.

3. No change shall be made in the outside appearance of Clay Cottage.''

Schedules are used in printed forms of common instruments, such as leases, mortgages or deeds of settlement for discretionary trusts. The printed form identifies important, and variable, elements as being set out in a schedule. The names of the parties, the date of the instrument and, for example, in the case of a mortgage, the sum of money lent, the date of repayment of the loan, the date from which interest is computed, rate of interest, dates for interest payments and a description of the mortgaged land are inserted in the schedule. Preparation of a document in this manner has two advantages. It is easy to prepare, as often only one page needs to be filled in. To a person familiar with the form, the purport of the document may be quickly grasped by reading the schedule. Some transactions are stereotyped and lend themselves to a printed document. The printed form will have been designed to have a particular legal effect. The propounder of the document may be reluctant to amend the text and may confine drafting activities to the schedule. This may hinder the expression of the common intentions of the parties.

Repetition of prepositions

Care must be taken in the use of prepositions before the items of a series of particulars. A gift:

to the chidren of A and B

A and B not being husband and wife—is in strict construction a gift to B and to the children of A, although the context may show a different intention.[8] If the children of B are to share, and not B himself, the gift should be framed:

to the children of A and to the children of B

or

to the children of A and of B

or, more colloquially,

to A's children and B's children.

Such gifts give rise to a further difficulty, that is, to determine whether the beneficiaries take shares determined per stirpes[9] or per capita. Prima facie words such as those in the above examples

8. *Re Dale* [1931] 1 Ch 357, 367; *Re Birkett* [1950] Ch 330. See also article "Prepositions in Enumeration" in (1933) 6 ALJ 444.
9. By stocks or families. Per stirpes expresses succinctly a concept which would require many more words to express in English.

import division per capita, and the word "between" does not now indicate a division into two.[10] The doubts which may arise are, however, considerable, and Sargant J in *Re Harper*[11] said, "Decisions in cases of this kind are necessarily rather in the nature of guesswork." Consequently, it is far better to state the shares in which the beneficiaries are to take, for instance, if a distribution per stirpes is intended,

> **in trust to divide the trust fund into two equal shares and to hold one share in trust for such of the children of A as are living at my death and attain the age of eighteen years and to hold the other share in trust for such of the children of B etc.**

The absence of an "of" resulted in judicial differences about the correct construction of s 104(5) of the *English Agriculture Act 1947*:

> **No officer or servant of a county agricultural executive committee, or any sub-committee or district committee thereof, shall be appointed .... to receive representations.**

The Court of Appeal in *R v Minister of Agriculture and Fisheries; Ex parte Graham*[12] decided that the subsection should be read as if the word "of" were inserted before "any". That was undoubtedly the intention of the legislature; it would have been unreasonable to enact that an officer of a subcommittee could be appointed but not an officer of the executive committee. Nevertheless, the omission of the second preposition caused a serious ambiguity and led the Divisional Court (whose judgment was overruled by the Court of Appeal) to hold that the subsection must be read as if it said that no subcommittee or district committee should be appointed to receive representations.

If the preposition consists of more than one word it may be better to repeat each of them, as in:

> **The amount of the substituted pension shall be *according to* the age of the nominated beneficiary on her birthday nearest to the date of the member's attainment of normal pension age**

10. *Re Walbran* [1906] 1 Ch 64; *Re Prosser* [1929] WN 85; *Re Alcock* [1945] Ch 264 at 269; *Conveyancer's Year Book* (1946), Vol 7, p 221; *Re Birkett* [1950] Ch 330.
11. [1914] 1 Ch 70 at 76.
12. [1955] 2 QB 140.

and *according to* the extent to which the amount of the monthly instalment of pension payable during the joint lives is reduced after the first death.

where, with "to" occurring several times, the repetition of "according" makes the meaning plainer.

The phrase:

Gifts made by a member and her husband

illustrates the difficulty that can arise from using prepositions carelessly. Does this mean gifts made by the member and her husband jointly? If it does, the word "jointly" should be added at the end of the phrase to avoid doubt. If gifts by either of them are meant:

Gifts made by a member or her husband

is suitable.

Resuming words

If a sentence commences with a statement of a case or condition,[13] it may clarify the meaning to put in a resuming word before the statement of the subject and the legal result, as:

If the foregoing trusts in favour of my children and grandchildren fail, *then* during the life of my husband my trustee shall hold etc.

in which "then" serves also the purpose of separating "fail" from "during the life of my husband".

Again, if a number of particulars have been stated, followed by the legal consequence, the latter may be introduced by "then, in any such event". For instance:

If—

    (a) a director resigns, or

    (b) a resolution is passed by which a director is removed from office, or

    (c) a director is absent without leave from more than three consecutive meetings,

then, in any such event, etc.

---

13. For meaning of *case* and *conditions* see above, pp 31-33.

Attempted repetition

If a class is referred to as as in a trust for:

> **such of the children of A as are living at the death of the Settlor or are born at any time afterwards who being male attain the age of 18 years or being female attain that age or marry . . .**

and there is a further disposition upon failure of those trusts, the circumstances on which the further disposition is to take effect could be described in these terms:

> **but if there is no child of A who is alive at the Settlor's death or born at any time afterwards who being male attains the age of 18 years or being female attains that age or marries then upon trust . . .**

This method is wordy and can cause uncertainty if the circumstances under which the further disposition is to take place are, through inadvertence, not accurately stated. It is preferable to use one of these formulae:

> **but, if no child of A attains a vested interest, then upon trust . . .**

> **but, in the event of the failure of those trusts, then upon trust . . .**

Enumerating particulars and excluding the "Ejusdem Generis" Rule

Sir Alison Russell[14] recommends:

> "Whenever possible it is best to avoid the enumeration of a number of particulars, since it is difficult to make that enumeration complete, and omissions may lead to the question whether, as the omissions were not included in the enumeration, they must be deemed to have been expressly omitted."

It is not safe to attempt to cure this difficulty merely be inserting general words to follow specific words.

> "As a rule, general words following specific words of the genus or category take their meaning from them and are

14. Russell (1938), p 106.

restricted to the same genus or category as the specific words which precede them."

So in a bill of lading which contained an exception in the words "should entry and discharge at a port be deemed by the master unsafe in consequence of war, disturbance or any other cause", it was held in *SS Knutsford Ltd v Tillmans & Co*[15] that the words "or any other cause" must be read as being ejusdem generis with war or disturbance, and that the exception did not cover a case where the master deemed the port unsafe or inaccessible on account of ice.

Russell recommends that when a list of things which are of the same genus or category ends with the words "or any other . . .", and it is intended that the ejusdem generis rule should not apply, some such phrase as the following should be used:

> **or any other . . . whether of the same kind as those . . . previously listed or not.**

A difficulty of an opposite kind occurs where general words are followed by particular items:

> **I give to X the contents of my home, including, in particular, my furniture, furnishings, linen, glassware, cutlery, crockery and kitchenware.**

This passage might provide an argument for cutting down the generality of the expression "the contents of my home" by reference to the particular items. It could be argued that the gift was intended to be restricted to items of domestic use. Leaving aside the question of whether such an expression as "the contents of my home" could ever be made precise, a method of preventing an enumeration of particulars from cutting down the meaning of a general term is by the insertion (after "in particular" in the above passage) of:

> **"without limiting (affecting) the generality of the foregoing".**[16]

Another device is to introduce the list of specific items by

> **"including, but not limited to".**

---

15. [1908] AC 406.
16. The meaning of the words "in particular" is doubtful. They are normally used to remove doubt as to whether a specific example falls within an earlier general phrase but they may not have the same meaning as "for example" or "and also": *Earl Fitzwilliam's Wentworth Estates Co v Minister of Housing and Local Government* [1952] AC 362.

Marginal notes and cross headings

Marginal notes assist quick reference. They are an aid to the reader in any document of appreciable length.

Cross headings are not used in short documents. If the document is long, it can be divided into numbered parts with appropriate titles, and these in turn can have divisions with cross headings.

One precaution should always be kept in mind when marginal notes are used in the draft of a document that is not already at its final stage. During discussion of a draft, or in the successive stages it may go through, changes are likely to be made. Some of these may necessitate alteration of marginal notes, or even of cross headings, and these should not be overlooked in the final check. A provision, such as this, can be put in the interpretation clause:

Cross headings and marginal notes are for reference purposes only and do not affect the interpretation of this document.

Numbering of clauses altered

Cross references in a document are usually made by referring to a provision by number (or other designation). To facilitate correction of references if the original numbering is changed, the numbers in the text by which other provisions are referred to can be marked or highlighted. The same precautions can be taken with such a reference as to "the last preceding clause" in case another clause is placed between them.

Checking the draft

However careful a drafter may be, an occasional mistake may be made. One safeguard is to put aside a finished draft at least until the next day; faults may be found that were not apparent when the document was first prepared. If there is time it is better to put it aside until it is almost forgotten; the drafter will then be almost as good a critic as a stranger who has not seen it before. But the best course is to have it considered and checked from end to end by someone else. Often these ideals are, unfortunately, unattainable.

An aid against error in matters of fact is the checking by the drafter of figures, names, places and the like, each of which should be noted on the draft with, for example, a pencil tick when it has been checked.

11
Expressions Relating to Time

This chapter shows the care needed in framing provisions in which time is relevant. Stipulations as to the time by or within which an act must be performed, the date of commencement or expiration of a tenancy, the period for which default must continue before a remedy is available, the length of a notice: these and similar expressions must be precise and clear. The clients should not be in doubt about what their rights are or how and when they may be exercised.

"On"

If a period of time is stated to begin on a named day, that day is included.[1] "On and from" or "on and after" a day includes that day.[2] A year "commencing on" 1 May ends on the next 30 April.

In the South Australian case of *Blackett v Clutterbuck Bros (Adelaide) Ltd*,[3] it was decided that a contract to deliver goods "on or about 1 October" was not performed by delivery on 2 September. Murray CJ said "a day or two on either side or perhaps three . . . would . . . be the most that could reasonably be held to be covered by the expression".

In *Dagger v Shepherd*,[4] the Court of Appeal decided that a notice to a tenant to quit "on or before" a specified date was valid, its effect being to give the tenant notice of termination of the

1. *Sidebotham v Holland* [1895] 1 QB 378.
2. Ibid at 384.
3. [1923] SASR 301.
4. [1946] KB 215.

tenancy on the specified date and to offer the tenant the opportunity to accept termination on an earlier date chosen by her or him.

"From" a date or event

Questions often occur as to the commencement of a period defined as "from" a date or event. Although on referring to the authorities it may be possible to answer the question, it is better to avoid it from the beginning.

The now repealed s 44 of the Victorian *Instruments Act* 1958 provided that:

> **"every bill of sale . . . shall at the expiration of twelve months from the filing thereof . . . become null and void unless within that time an affidavit is filed. . . ."**

In *Stearns v Klug*,[5] it was held that an affidavit of renewal filed on the corresponding date of the year succeeding that in which a previous affidavit of renewal had been filed was filed within the time limited by the section.

It has been said by Mathew LJ that "The rule is now well established that where a particular time is given, from a certain date, within which an act is to be done, the day of the date is to be excluded".[6] The period defined by "from the date of this deed for three years" would therefore not include the date of the deed, and the first day of the three years would be the day following that date.

In *Associated Beauty Aids Pty Ltd v FCT*,[7] a shareholder was entitled, by notice to the company, to convert his preference shares to ordinary shares "whereupon the shares so specified shall from the date of delivery of the notice become ordinary shares." It was held that the conversion took effect on the day following the day of delivery of the notice.

In *English v Cliff*,[8] Warrington J said there was no absolute rule with regard to the inclusion or exclusion of the day on which a particular event takes place; it was a matter to be determined

5. (1895) 21 VLR 164.
6. *Goldsmith's Co v West Metropolitan Railway* [1904] 1 KB 1 at 5; *South Staffordshire Tramways Co v Sickness & Accident Assurance Co* [1891] 1 QB 402; *Stewart v Chapman* [1951] 2 KB 792.
7. (1965) 113 CLR 662.
8. [1914] 2 Ch 376.

from the particular deed. In that case a period of "twenty-one years *from* the date of these presents" was held, in the context, to include the day on which the deed was executed. Similarly, in the Canadian decision *West v Barr*,[9] where a lease was expressed to commence "from" a certain date it was held that the context must be examined in order to determine the sense in which the word was used.[10]

In *Forster v Jododex (Australia) Pty Ltd*,[11] the High Court decided that where time is computed from a date, prima facie that date is excluded from the period. Gibbs J said:

"Where a written instrument requires a period of time to be computed 'from' a specified date, it depends on the true construction of the instrument whether the date specified is to be included in the period. Generally speaking, however, the day from which the period runs is excluded, although there is no rigid rule to that effect and 'from' is capable of having an inclusive effect in an appropriate context."

The doubts that can arise in the construction of stipulations as to time, not only those already mentioned but those referred to later in this chapter, show that it is essential to express the intention of the parties clearly. In the *Forster* case the question whether an application for renewal was made not later than one month before the expiry of a licence was decided by the High Court and the court divided three judges to two. The client suffers a gross disservice if, because of imprecise drafting, the meaning of the document requires elucidation by a court.

It has been said that the computation of time from the doing of an act, such as the giving of a notice, commences the moment the act is done whereas the computation of time from the day on which an act is done commences on the next day.[12]

The different meanings of the expressions:

"15 days from the date of commencement of risk"

and

"15 days from commencement of risk"

9. [1945] 1 WWR 337.
10. *Ackland v Lutley* (1839) 9 Ad & E 879; *Meggeson v Groves* [1917] 1 Ch 158.
11. (1972) 127 CLR 421 at 440, per Gibbs J.
12. *Howard's Case* (1699) 2 Salk 625; 91 ER 528.

was discussed in *Cartwright v MacCormack; Trafalgar Insurance Co Ltd*.[13] The former period of 15 days commences at midnight at the end of the day of commencement; the latter period at the time of day at which the risk commences.

Instead of

from the date of this deed

it is better to say that the period commences on a specified date which can, of course, be the date of the deed or the next day after the date of the deed.

But in a mortgage it is usual to state that interest is to commence from a named date; the rule then is that that date is not included in calculating the interest.

"*Commencing with*" and "*ending with*" a named day are expressions which leave no doubt that the day named in either case is included in the period. In *Hare v Goucher*,[14] a period was defined as "beginning with" a certain day and accordingly that day was included in computing the period.

In *Trow v Ind Coope (West Midlands) Ltd*,[15] the Court of Appeal had to determine whether a writ issued on 10 September 1965 could be validly served on 10 September 1966. The rule of court read: "For the purpose of service, a writ . . . is valid in the first instance for twelve months beginning with the date of its issue. . . ." A majority of the court considered that the period of 12 months expired on 9 September 1966. It was also held that an indorsement on the writ: "This writ may not be served more than twelve months after (the date of its issue) . . ." implied that the writ could be effectively served on 10 September 1966. The view was expressed that the words "beginning with," quoted above, were indistinguishable from "commencing on".

"After" and "Within"

If a period of two months is to expire after an event before something must be done, the date of that event is not included.[16]

13. [1963] 1 WLR 18; [1963] 1 All ER 11 (CA).
14. [1962] 2 QB 641.
15. [1967] 2 All ER 900.
16. *Blunt v Heslop* (1838) 8 Ad & E 577; 112 ER 957; *Browne v Black* [1912] 1 KB 316.

"Within" seven days after an event, also, usually does not include the day of the happening of the event; if that day is the 6th, the period ends at midnight of the 13th/14th.[17] The Victorian Full Court has stated the rule in respect of statutes as follows:[18]

> "The modern rule in relation to a period of time fixed by statute within which an act is to be done after a specified event is that the day of the event is to be excluded; the next day is the first day of the stipulated period and the time expires on the last day of the period, counting from and of course including the first day."

But it is better to avoid any doubt. Use a phrase that shows precisely when the period begins:

The arbitrator shall make his award *within the period of* **two months** *commencing on* **the day of (or the day after) his appointment.**

As a statute commences immediately after the expiration of the day preceding that on which the statute is assented to or proclaimed to commence, to say that "after the commencement" of an Act something may be done or may not be done would usually mean that at any time after the expiration of the previous day it might or might not be done.

If the date of commencement of a period mentioned in a document is known, say 1 May, it may be better to say that "on and after" 1 May something may or may not be done; if you have to distinguish the period before the commencement you may say "on or before 30 April".

"From and after" a date multiplies words but does not increase clarity.

"After" and "before" can be used with reference to one date in such a way as to exclude the date on a strict interpretation of the language used:

If, before 15 August . . .

If, after 15 August. . . .

The expression "between (two dates)" can also cause difficulty, because the interval of time begins immediately after the earlier date and ends immediately before the later date. The period

17. *Williams v Burgess* (1840) 10 LJQB 10; 113 ER 955.
18. *Morton v Hampson* [1962] VR 364 at 365.

between 1 July 1985 and 30 June 1986 does not, strictly interpreted, include either 1 July or 30 June. A more liberal interpretation might be held to be correct but the meaning should be made quite clear.

If an act may be done before a specified event, or within a specified time after that event, both conditions are not expressed by

"within six months after the termination of the tenancy";

but both are expressed by

"not later than six months after the termination of the tenancy"

or, of course, by the statement of each condition in the form

"before the termination of the tenancy or within six months after its termination".

"Till" and "until" a day

These are ambiguous as to whether the day named is or is not included. A stay of execution granted "until May 1 next" has been held not to prevent issue on that day,[19] but a fire policy which insured goods "from the 14th day of February 1868 until the 14th day of August 1868" was held to protect them during the whole of 14 August.[20] The drafter should not use "till" and "until" without some addition if there is any room for doubt:

until and including 1 May next,

or, if 1 May is not included,

until but not including 1 May next,

or

until and including 30 April next.

"To" also is ambiguous. In referring to the period of which 1 January is the first day and 6 February the last this expression is ambiguous:

from 1 January to 6 February;

but these expressions

from 1 January to 6 February, both days included

---

19. *Rogers v Davis* (1845) 8 Ir LR 399.
20. *Isaacs v Royal Insurance Co* (1870) LR 5 Exch 296.

and

commencing on 1 January and ending on 6 February

are free from ambiguity.

"By a day"

If an act is required to be done "by" a specified date, performance on or at any time before that date is sufficient. A notice to vacate premises "by" a date stated, being a date on which the periodic tenancy is liable to be determined, is valid.[21] In *J H Munro Ltd v Vancouver Properties Ltd*,[22] the Court of Appeal of British Columbia decided that a tenant who was given notice to quit "by 31 July" might remain in possession throughout the whole of that day.

"At the expiration of" was held, in construing a statute, to mean "at or after the expiration of".[23] The decision depended on the context and on special circumstances. In other contexts, the intention of the parties might best be expressed by specifying the actual day on which the period expired.

"Day"

A day, except in the sense of contradistinction from night, is a period of 24 consecutive hours—usually from midnight to the following midnight, but it may mean 24 hours commencing at any hour. If there can be any doubt, it should be made clear which is intended. Whether a fraction of a day is to be included in a period is often the occasion of doubt; the answer appears to depend on intention and the context of the statute or document in question.[24] Many of the cases are reviewed in *Belfield v Belfield*,[25] in which O'Bryan J held that where desertion had commenced on the evening of 2 March 1942, and a petition for divorce was filed on the afternoon of 2 March 1945, the statutory period of desertion "during three years and upwards" had not been completed when

21. *Easthaugh v Macpherson* [1954] 1 WLR 1307.
22. [1940] 3 WWR 26.
23. *In the goods of Ruddy* (1872) LR 2 P & D 330.
24. *Re North; Ex parte Hasluck* [1895] 2 QB 264; *Wilkie v Inland Revenue Commissioners* [1952] Ch 153.
25. [1945] VLR 231.

the petition was filed. The words "thirty days" in a policy insurance may, to give effect to the apparent intention of the parties, be construed as meaning 30 consecutive periods of 24 hours and not 30 calendar days.[26]

If the drafter wishes a period to be measured in whole days, the period should be stated to commence on or with a specified or ascertainable day, not a specified or ascertainable time. The use of the word "time" may lead to the inference that the period is to be measured from or to an exact time of day.[27]

"The first day of each week" in a tenancy agreement was, in *Love v Chryssoulis*,[28] held, in the absence of context to the contrary, to mean the first day of each week of the tenancy and not to have its dictionary meaning of Sunday.

"Clear day" means a period of 24 hours commencing at midnight. "Within ten clear days after 1 January" means the period commencing at midnight of 1/2 January and ending at midnight on 11/12 January.

"Not less than" a specified number of days

Chitty J, in *Re Railway Sleepers Supply Co*,[29] said that the words "not less than fourteen days" meant an interval of at least 14 clear days, as the phrase is equivalent to saying that 14 days must intervene or elapse between the two dates. Similarly, in *Re Hector Whaling Ltd*[30] Bennet J held that, where not less than 21 days' notice of a meeting was required, those days were clear days, exclusive of the day of service of the notice and of the day of the meeting. This decision has been followed in England[31] but there is a contrary Scottish decision.[32] Although the general rule is that such a period of time must be calculated inclusive of one of the days and exclusive of the other, the courts have frequently construed such provisions as to time, particularly in statutes, as referring to "clear days". So it is advisable to state whether or not "clear" days are intended.

26. *Cornfoot v Royal Exchange Assurance Corp* [1904] 1 KB 40.
27. See above, pp 115-116 and Dickerson (1965), pp 93-94.
28. (1977) 16 ACTR 1.
29. (1885) 29 Ch D 204.
30. [1936] 1 Ch 208.
31. *Thompson v Stimpson* [1961] 1 QB 195.
32. *Neil McLeod & Sons Ltd Petitioners* 1967 SC 16.

"Within seven clear days after" the 6th means the same as "within seven days after" the 6th; the period ends at midnight of the 13th/14th.[33]

"Month"

At common law, "month" meant lunar month[34] unless it fell within one of the recognised exceptions.

In *Phipps & Co v Rogers*,[35] Atkin LJ commented on the common law meaning of "month":

> **The result is to adopt a meaning which is nearly always contrary to the intention of the parties. The rule is fortunately almost destroyed by exceptions. It does not apply to mercantile contracts or to statutes or to mortgages or to cases where the context requires the meaning of calendar month. It never did apply in ecclesiastical law. In the residue of cases, it clearly does apply as is established by a series of authorities which we cannot overrule. I am clearly of the opinion that it is a public disadvantage that the rule should continue.**

"Month", in any deed, contract, will, order or other instrument is, in most jurisdictions, now defined by statute[36] to mean, unless the context otherwise requires, "calendar month". Because lay-people may not be aware of this statutory provision, it is sometimes recommended that a month should be stated to be a calendar month if, in fact, this is intended. However, most people today would regard "month" as being equivalent to "calendar month".

If a lunar month is intended, the phrase "a period of twenty-eight days" (or "four weeks") is preferable.

The general rule is that a period of a calendar month after the occurrence of an event commences at midnight of the day on which the event occurs and ends at midnight on the same day of the next month.[37] If there is no such day, it ends at midnight on the last

---

33. *Armstrong v Great Southern Gold Mining Co* (1911) 12 CLR 382 at 388.
34. *Kodak v Hally* [1960] Qd R 452; *Development Underwriting (Qld) Pty Ltd v Weaber* [1971] Qd R 182.
35. [1925] 1 KB 14 at 26-27.
36. See above, p 52.
37. *McPherson v Lawless* [1960] VR 363.

day of the next month. In *Dodds v Walker*[38] a period of four months after 30 September was held to expire on 30 January in the next year, not 31 January. Expressions involving calendar months need to be carefully considered. Their construction will depend on the context and the circumstances.

"Year"

Year means "a period of 12 calendar months calculated either from 1 January or some other named day and consists of 365 days in an ordinary year, and 366 days if the period includes 29 February in a leap year".[39]

In *Re Clubb*,[40] Burchett J held that a bank was in error when it calculated interest for a period in a year of 366 days on the assumption that the year contained 365 days.

Reference to date

A date in a legal document is often stated as: the 15th day of May. It is sufficient to use "15th May" or "May 15". No one could imagine that the parties intended to refer to the 15th hour, minute or second of the month. Where dates are left blank in a document and are to be subsequently inserted, the use of "the   day of   19—" facilitates correct completion of the date, even if it looks cumbersome. "15 May 1994" is a more logical order than "May 15 1994".

Expressions of recurrence

Useful phrases are *when and as often as* (which Russell prefers to "whenever" for conveying the meaning of recurrence) and *if and so long as*.

Anniversary is useful for defining successive periods of one year, as in "any period of six months commencing on the date of this agreement, or on the date six months after that date, or on any *anniversary* of either of those dates."

38. [1981] 1 WLR 1027 (HL); *Migotti v Colvill* (1879) 4 CPD 233.
39. Odgers (1967), p 126.
40. (1990) 93 ALR 123.

"Within a reasonable time"

Whenever possible, it is better to fix a time in which an act must be done, and not to refer to a "reasonable time", because there may be a dispute as to what is reasonable. In *Stickney v Keeble*,[41] the question whether a period of notice was reasonable was eventually decided by the House of Lords. Nevertheless, the law implies that many acts will be done in a reasonable time, and so the words may be used in a contract.

In deciding whether performance has taken place within a reasonable time, time may be extended beyond its normal span by special circumstances, and these may include circumstances which did not exist at the time of the contract, but which supervene later, hampering performance.[42]

"Forthwith", "immediately"

"The words 'forthwith' and 'immediately' have the same meaning. They are stronger than the expression 'within a reasonable time', and imply prompt, vigorous action, without any delay, and whether there has been such action is a question of fact, having regard to the circumstances of the particular case."[43]

The meaning ascribed to the words will depend on the context in which they are used.[44] "Forthwith" has in other cases been held to mean "at once, having regard to the circumstances of the case", "with as little delay as possible", "without delay or loss of time".[45] "There appears to be no material difference between the terms 'immediately' and 'forthwith'. A provision to the effect that a thing must be done 'forthwith' or 'immediately' means that it must be done as soon as possible in the circumstances, the nature of the act to be done being taken into account."[46]

41. [1915] AC 386.
42. *Monkland v Jack Barclay* [1951] 2 KB 252 at 259 per Asquith LJ. See also 63 ALJ 131.
43. *R v Berkshire Justices* (1879) 4 QBD 469 at 471.
44. *Drymalik v Feldman* [1966] SASR 227.
45. *Measures v McFadyen* (1910) 11 CLR 723 at 736.
46. Halsbury (4th ed), Vol 45, p 553, para 1148. *London Borough of Hillingdon v Cutler* [1967] 2 All ER 361.

"Forthwith", in relation to payment of a deposit under a contract of sale, was held in *Hill v Sidney*[47] to mean as soon as is reasonably practicable or reasonably possible.

An action required to be carried out "forthwith" following an earlier action need not necessarily be on the same day.[48] It is clear that the use of any of these expressions may bring the parties into court if they do not agree. It is preferable to state the period within which the act must be done if the period can be agreed upon.

"As soon as possible"

When used in a contract these words mean that the act promised will be done within a reasonable time and undertake that it will be done in the shortest practicable time.[49] In determining what is commercially possible, surrounding circumstances may be considered, but the limited resources of the contracting party are not relevant.[50] Consequently, a party to a contract should think carefully before undertaking to do something "as soon as possible". The interpretation of this imperative term can be affected by its context[51] or the surrounding circumstances.[52]

47. [1991] 2 Qd R 547.
48. *Fernando v Nikulan Appu* (1920) 22 NLR 1; *Sameen v Abeyewickrema* [1963] AC 597.
49. *Hydraulic Engineering Co v McHaffie* (1878) 4 QBD 670; this decision was followed in the Canadian case, *Kings Old Country Ltd v Liquid Carbonic Canadian Corp Ltd* [1942] 2 WWR 603.
50. *Hydraulic Engineering Co v McHaffie* (1878) 4 QBD 670; *Verelest's Administratrix v Motor Union Insurance Co Ltd* [1925] 2 KB 137.
51. *Vines v Djordjevitch* [1955] ALR 431 at 435.
52. *Amann Aviation v Commonwealth* (1990) 92 ALR 601 at 632-633.

Index